Meadowbrook
Quilts

Martingale®
& COMPANY

Meadowbrook Quilts

12 Projects

Inspired by Nature

Jean Van Bockel

Meadowbrook Quilts:
12 Projects Inspired by Nature
© 2003 by Jean Van Bockel

Martingale & Company
20205 144th Avenue NE
Woodinville, WA 98072-8478
www.martingale-pub.com

Printed in China
08 07 06 05 04 03   8 7 6 5 4 3 2 1

Library of Congress Cataloging-in-Publication Data
Van Bockel, Jean.
    Meadowbrook quilts : 12 projects inspired by nature
/ Jean Van Bockel.
        p. cm.
    ISBN 1-56477-493-7
    1. Patchwork—Patterns. 2. Appliqué—Patterns.
3. Quilting. 4. Nature in art. I. Title.
    TT835 .V353 2003
    746 .46 ' 041—dc21
                            2003013857

Mission Statement
Dedicated to providing quality products
and service to inspire creativity.

Credits
President: Nancy J. Martin
CEO: Daniel J. Martin
Publisher: Jane Hamada
Editorial Director: Mary V. Green
Managing Editor: Tina Cook
Technical Editor: Cyndi Hershey
Copy Editor: Melissa Bryan
Design Director: Stan Green
Illustrator: Laurel Strand
Cover and Text Designer: Regina Girard
Photographer: Brent Kane

Acknowledgements

With thanks and appreciation to:

✳ My husband, Mark; daughters Wren and Kitty; and son Miles for their great support and honest feedback.

✳ My son-in-law Jay, who saved me many hours of work with his computer knowledge.

✳ Pam Mostek, who took time out of her busy schedule to look over and finesse my writing.

✳ Joanne Case, for her spectacular quilting designs and for quilting all of the large quilt projects.

✳ My sister, Kathy White, who helped appliqué many leaves and roses.

✳ Hoffman Fabrics, for supplying the batik fabrics used in "Wild Roses."

✳ The efficient staff at Martingale & Company, and Cyndi Hershey and Melissa Bryan for their editing expertise.

Contents

Introduction

For the past thirteen years, I have walked a beautiful route behind our house in the countryside of northern Idaho. My walk takes me up a steep hill through the woods and then out into picturesque farmland surrounded by lush forested mountains on a trail called Meadowbrook Loop.

I try to get out each day, with a little help from our Australian shepherd who faithfully prods me away from the sewing machine. I'm always glad that he coaxes me into it, because these walks are my inspiration. This is where the ideas for *Meadowbrook Quilts* were born. It was a cold January morning when I came home and pulled out my box of recycled wool scraps. I wanted to make a warm quilt with the subtle shades of the snow-blown fields and the cold winter land-scape that I had just seen on my walk. This was the beginning of "Winter Morning," the wool quilt on page 62.

From that first inspi-ration, my collection of ideas from my daily walks began to grow and develop. I wanted to capture the fresh, new color palette that sur-prised me the day after a warm, windy evening melted the hillside snow.

And the sight of the tree swal-lows as they return from their long journey, dipping and soar-ing through the gusty April skies, had to be captured too.

The strong, delicious fra-grance of the wild rose—which I could enjoy before I actually saw the lovely pink petals—inspired me to cre-ate a delicate rose-appliquéd quilt. And then there is my rock collection. Many days I returned with stone-stuffed pockets, and this was the start of "Sticks and Stones" on page 44.

The ideas were limit-less. Each day as I returned from my walk I had more and more inspirations I wanted to share. As you leaf through the pages of this book, you'll find the nature-inspired quilts that began on my daily route through the wooded countryside. I hope you will enjoy making them.

Or maybe the next time you experi-ence nature's special beauty you, too, will want to save that memory in a quilt of your own design. It may be a chirping bird, a delicate flower, or the blast of cold wind that stirs the creative talent within. Whatever it is, enjoy your walk!

Jean

Changing Leaves

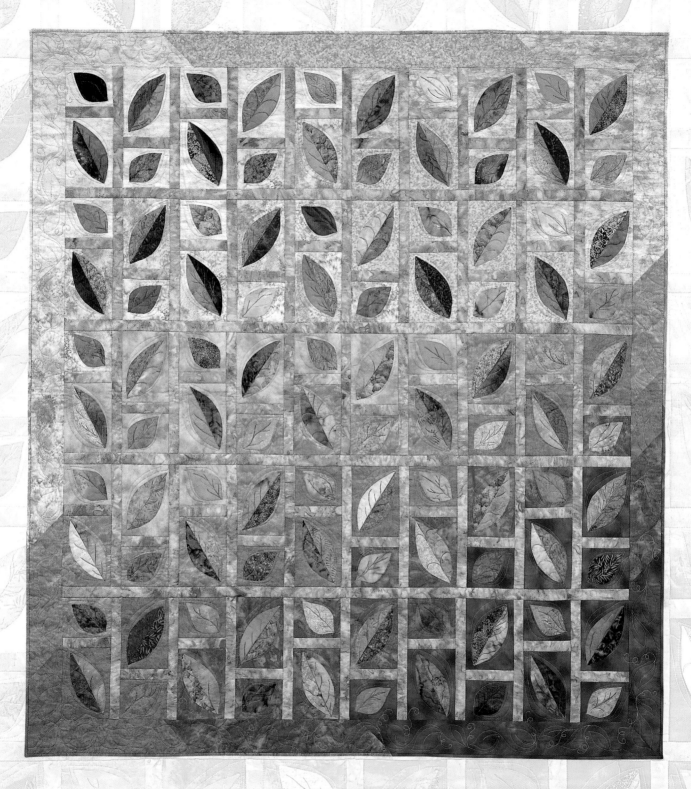

Finished Size: 65½" x 70½"

Finished Block Size: 12" x 12"

*Capture the colors of the leaves and sky as they travel through
the seasons, from the fresh shades of spring to the golden
tones of autumn. With invisible machine appliqué for
the leaves, this quilt is quick and easy to make.*

Materials

Yardages are based on 42"-wide fabric.

2 yards total of assorted leaf fabrics

1½ yards of tan fabric for sashing

⅝ yard of 9 different sky fabrics gradating from light blue to dark blue for blocks, borders, and binding

4 yards of fabric for backing (pieced horizontally)

70" x 75" piece of batting

Bias Square ruler or any ruler with a 45°-angle mark

Freezer paper

Cutting

All measurements include ¼" seam allowances.

From *each* of the 9 sky fabrics, cut:
- 2 strips, 5½" x 42"; crosscut into 6 rectangles, 5½" x 7½", and 6 rectangles, 5½" x 4½". You'll cut a total of 108 rectangles and will have 8 left over after piecing the quilt top.
- 1 strip, 3½" x 42"
- 1 strip, 2" x 42"

From the tan sashing fabric, cut:
- 30 strips, 1½" x 42"; crosscut into 50 rectangles, 1½" x 5½", and 45 rectangles, 1½" x 12½". The remaining strips will be used for creating horizontal sashing.

From the assorted leaf fabrics, cut:
- 50 rectangles, 3¼" x 5"
- 100 rectangles, 2" x 7½"

Making the Blocks

1. Place the sky fabric rectangles on your design wall or floor to gradate from the lightest blue in the top left corner down to the darkest blue in the bottom right corner. Lay out the rectangles in their block formation as shown, but you can wait to add the sashing when you sew the blocks.

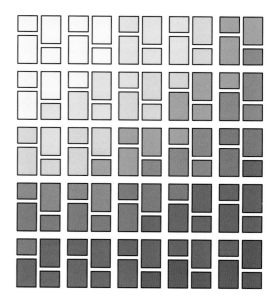

2. When you are pleased with the block layout, start sewing the sashing pieces to each block one at a time, replacing each block on your design wall as you sew. Sew the pieces as shown. Always press toward the sashing strip.

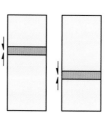 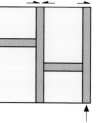

Leave this strip off the end blocks.

Adding the Appliqué

1. Sew the 2" x 7½" leaf rectangles together into pairs down the long side of the strips. Coordinate the colors so that you have a variety of leaves.

2. Trace the large and small leaf patterns on page 15 onto freezer paper and cut them out.

3. Place the freezer-paper leaves (dull side down) onto the wrong side of a set of leaf rectangles. Align both points of the leaves with the seam and pin in place.

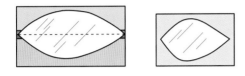

4. Refer to "Invisible Machine Appliqué" on page 86 for directions, and prepare and sew the leaf appliqués.

5. Referring to the quilt layout, place the leaves on the individual blocks. Place dark green leaves in the top left corner for contrast against the light blue sky. Sprinkle a few yellow leaves throughout the quilt and end with a few red-orange leaves in the dark autumn sky. When you are pleased with the arrangement, pin the leaves in place and machine appliqué.

Assembling the Quilt Top

1. Sew the blocks into five horizontal rows. Press toward the sashing.

2. Sew the 1½" x 42" tan sashing strips end to end. Press. From this long strip, cut four strips, 1½" x 59½". Sew these four strips between the five rows of blocks. Press toward the sashing.

3. Sew the rows together. Press toward the sashing.

Making the Borders

1. On the outside edge of your quilt top, measure between each color change in the background blocks. Add 4¼" to that measurement. Add 7" to the strips that meet in the corners to allow for mitered corners.

Upper left corner

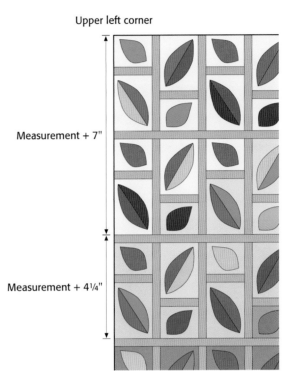

Measurement + 7"

Measurement + 4¼"

2. Using the above measurement, cut a strip from the 3½" x 42" corresponding sky fabric.

3. To cut adjoining border strips at 45° angles, stack the two strips with right sides facing up. Place the 45° line of the Bias Square ruler along the edge of the strips. Cut a 45° angle on the right end of the strips. Turn the bottom strip around so that the angles match. Continue to cut the rest of the border in the same manner.

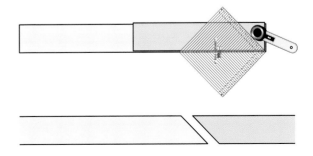

4. With right sides together, sew the border strips together. Offset the ends of the angles to allow an accurate ¼" seam.

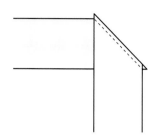

5. Referring to "Mitered Borders" on page 89, sew the borders to the quilt top.

Finishing Your Quilt

Refer to "General Directions," beginning on page 85, for specific directions regarding each of the following steps.

1. Layer the quilt top with batting and backing; baste.

2. Hand or machine quilt as desired. Quilting various veins on the leaves greatly enhances the visual effect.

3. Trim the batting and backing even with the quilt-top edges.

4. Measure between each color change on the border of the quilt. Cut 2" binding strips of sky fabric using this length plus 2¾" for angles and seam allowance. Add several inches to the first and last piece to allow for joining ends. Cut and sew the strips in the same way that you assembled the border strips, except you will sew the binding into one continuous strip. Following the directions for French binding, bind the quilt.

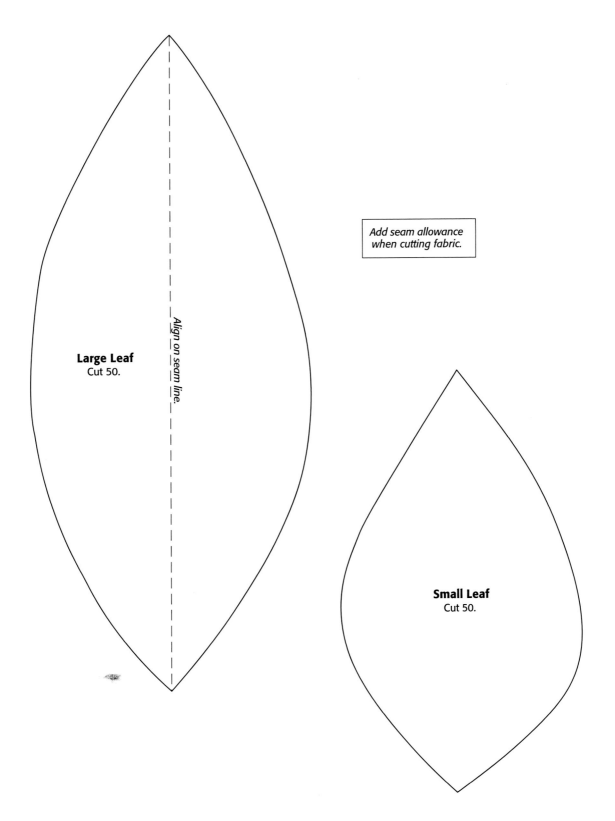

Add seam allowance
when cutting fabric.

Large Leaf
Cut 50.

Align on seam line.

Small Leaf
Cut 50.

Windblown Swallows

Finished Size: 44½" x 52½"
Finished Block Size: 8" x 8"

When the swallows return to the meadow nearby,
I imagine they've been blown home by a giant gust of
spring wind. Just like the swallows on this quilt, they
swoop and dive in a playful homecoming dance.

Materials

Yardages are based on 42"-wide fabric.

2¼ yards of sky fabric (nondirectional) for background and inner border

1⅜ yards of dark blue for blocks, outer border, and binding

1 yard of bright blue for blocks and border accent

¼ yard of navy blue for birds

Scrap of light gray for bird breasts

Scrap of medium gray for bird wings

Scrap of rusty red for bird throats

3⅛ yards of fabric for backing (pieced horizontally)

48" x 56" piece of batting

Embroidery floss in black and white

Freezer paper

Cutting

All measurements include ¼" seam allowances.

From the bright blue fabric, cut:

- 3 strips, 2½" x 42"; crosscut into 40 squares, 2½" x 2½"

- 2 strips, 4⅛" x 42"; crosscut into 10 squares, 4⅛" x 4⅛". Cut each square twice diagonally for a total of 40 quarter-square triangles.

- 2 strips, 5¼" x 42"; crosscut into 10 squares, 5¼" x 5¼". Cut each square twice diagonally for a total of 40 quarter-square triangles.

- 5 strips, 1" x 42"

From the dark blue fabric, cut:

- 3 strips, 2½" x 42"; crosscut into 40 squares, 2½" x 2½"

- 2 strips, 4⅛" x 42"; crosscut into 10 squares, 4⅛" x 4⅛". Cut each square twice diagonally for a total of 40 quarter-square triangles.

- 2 strips, 5¼" x 42"; crosscut into 10 squares, 5¼" x 5¼". Cut each square twice diagonally for a total of 40 quarter-square triangles.

- 5 strips, 1½" x 42"

- 5 strips, 2" x 42"

From the sky fabric, cut:

- 3 strips, 4½" x 42"; crosscut into 20 squares, 4½" x 4½"

- 3 strips, 4⅛" x 42"; crosscut into 20 squares, 4⅛" x 4⅛". Cut each square twice diagonally for a total of 80 quarter-square triangles.

- 3 strips, 5¼" x 42"; crosscut into 20 squares, 5¼" x 5¼". Cut each square twice diagonally for a total of 80 quarter-square triangles.

- 5 strips, 5½" x 42"

Making the Windblown Blocks

1. On the wrong side of the 2½" bright blue squares and the 2½" dark blue squares, draw a light pencil line diagonally from corner to corner. To mark on the fabric with ease, place the squares on the gritty side of a piece of fine-grain sandpaper so they won't slip while you draw.

2. With right sides together, place two bright blue squares on opposite corners of a 4½" sky square. Stitch on each line and cut off the corners, ¼" away from the stitching. Press toward the triangles.

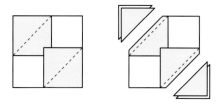

Make 20.

3. Place two dark blue squares on the remaining corners. Stitch on each line and cut off the corners, ¼" away from the stitching. Press toward the triangles.

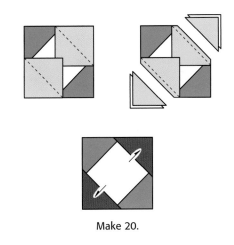

Make 20.

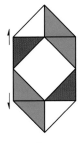

Make 20.

4. Sew the small bright blue triangles to the small sky triangles, sewing on the short side of the triangles so that the sky fabric is on the left when the unit is opened. Press toward the bright blue triangles.

Make 40.

5. Repeat step 4, sewing the small dark blue triangles to the remaining small sky triangles. Press toward the dark blue triangles.

6. Sew the bright blue triangle units from step 4 to the top and bottom of the center square units from step 3 as shown. Press toward the triangle units.

Make 20.

7. Sew the dark blue triangle units from step 5 to the remaining sides. Press toward the triangle units.

Make 20.

8. Sew the large bright blue triangles to the large sky triangles, sewing on the short side of the triangles so that the sky fabric is on the left when the unit is opened. Press toward the bright blue triangles.

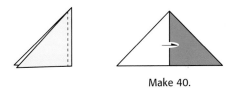

Make 40.

9. Repeat step 8, sewing the large dark blue triangles to the remaining large sky triangles.

10. Sew the bright blue triangle units from step 8 to opposite corners of the center block as shown. Press toward the triangle units.

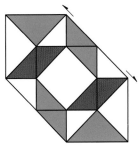

Make 20.

11. Sew the dark blue triangle units from step 9 to the remaining sides. Press toward the triangle units.

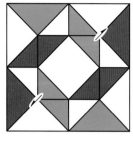

Make 20.

12. Arrange the blocks into five rows of four blocks each, positioning them so that alternating blocks are rotated as shown. Press the seams in opposite directions from row to row.

13. Sew the rows together. Press all seam allowances in the same direction.

Making the Borders

1. Referring to "Straight-Cut Borders" on page 89, use the 5½" sky fabric strips to add the inner border.

2. Sew the 1" bright blue accent strips end to end. Press seams open. From this strip, cut two strips 42½" long and two strips 50½" long.

3. Fold these accent strips in half lengthwise with wrong sides together and press.

4. With raw edges even and using a *scant* ¼" seam, sew the short strips to the top and bottom of the quilt. Leave strips folded in toward the center of the quilt. Sew the two long strips to the sides of the quilt and leave the strips folded in toward the quilt center.

5. Referring to "Straight-Cut Borders" on page 89, use the 1½" dark blue strips to add the outer border. Press these borders toward the accent strips.

Adding the Appliqué

1. Trace the pattern shapes on pages 22–23, referring to the directions for freezer-paper or needle-turn appliqué on page 85. Cut the required number of shapes from each appropriate fabric.

2. Refer to the quilt plan on page 21 for suggested placement of birds. Appliqué each piece in place in numerical order as shown on the templates.

3. Make the birds' eyes with French knots using three strands of black floss. Outline the eyes with a stem stitch using one strand of white floss.

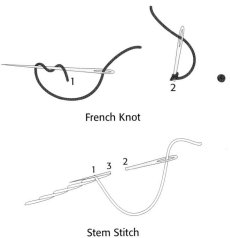

French Knot

Stem Stitch

Finishing Your Quilt

Refer to "General Directions," beginning on page 85, for specific directions regarding each of the following finishing steps.

1. Layer the quilt top with batting and backing; baste.

2. Machine or hand quilt as desired.

3. Trim the batting and backing even with the quilt-top edges.

4. Referring to "French Binding" on page 92, prepare the 2" dark blue strips for binding and sew the binding to the quilt.

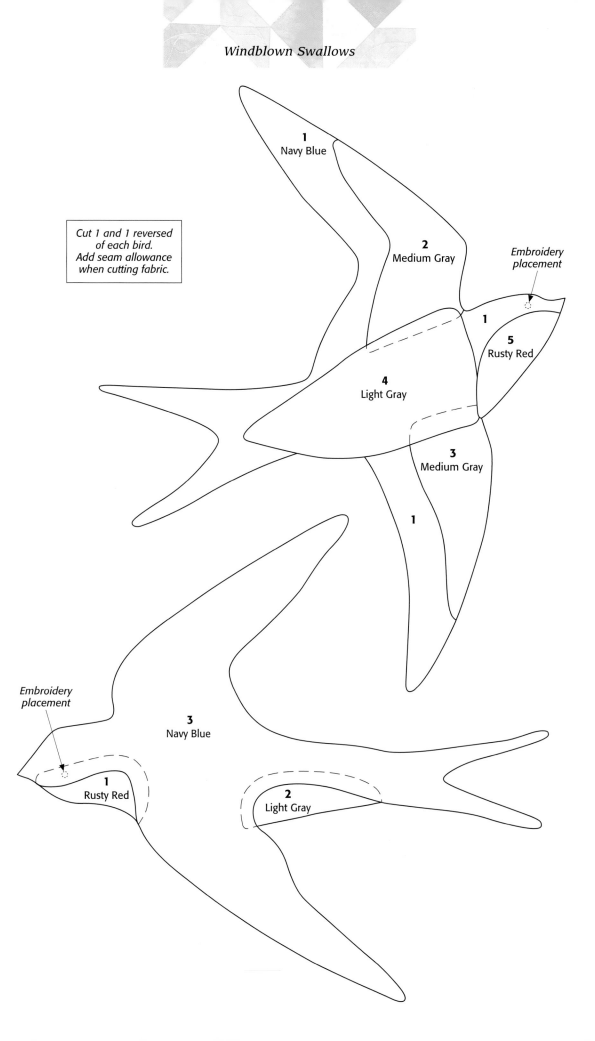

Cut 1 and 1 reversed
of each bird.
Add seam allowance
when cutting fabric.

1
Navy Blue

2
Medium Gray

*Embroidery
placement*

1

5
Rusty Red

4
Light Gray

3
Medium Gray

1

*Embroidery
placement*

3
Navy Blue

1
Rusty Red

2
Light Gray

22

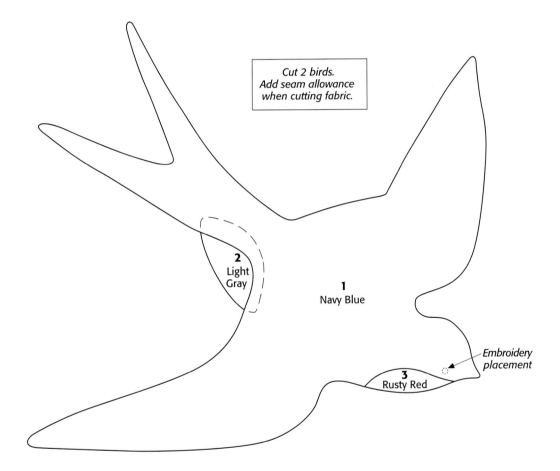

Cut 2 birds.
Add seam allowance
when cutting fabric.

2
Light
Gray

1
Navy Blue

3
Rusty Red

*Embroidery
placement*

Spring Wildflowers

Finished Size: 15¾" x 20"
Finished Block Size: 3" x 3"

*From early spring to midsummer, a multitude of colorful
wildflowers magically appear scattered throughout the
fields and forest. Re-creating those delightful blooms
on this wall quilt is easy to do with paper piecing.*

Materials

Yardages are based on 42"-wide fabric.

¾ yard of bright green print for background, border, and binding

¼ yard of floral print for flower centers*

¼ yard of dark green print for leaves and accent strips

⅛ yard each of 8 different petal fabrics: red, white, orange, light orange, dark purple, red-purple, yellow, and pink

½ yard of fabric for backing

18" x 22" piece of batting

Freezer paper

* *You will need to "fussy cut" 1½" squares for each flower center. Check repeats in fabric before purchasing yardage. You may want to use a variety of flower prints in order to match the petal color.*

Cutting

All measurements include ¼" seam allowances.

From the floral print, cut:

- 18 squares, 1½" x 1½", "fussy cutting" to center a motif within each one

From each of the 8 petal fabrics, cut:

- 2 strips, 1¼" x 42"; crosscut into 40 rectangles, 1¼" x 2"

From the bright green print, cut:

- 8 strips, 1½" x 42"; crosscut into 144 squares, 1½" x 1½". Cut each remaining strip into 2 strips, 1½" x 22", and 2 strips, 1½" x 18".

- 3 squares, 5½" x 5½"; cut twice diagonally for a total of 12 quarter-square triangles. (You will use only 10.)

- 2 squares, 3 " x 3"; cut once diagonally for a total of 4 half-square triangles

- 2 strips, 1¼" x 42"

From the dark green fabric, cut:

- 3 strips, ¾" x 42"; crosscut into 2 strips, ¾" x 22", and 2 strips, ¾" x 18"

Making the Blocks

If you are new to the paper-piecing technique, you might wish to read further details in an introductory book such as *Show Me How to Paper Piece* by Carol Doak (Martingale & Company, 1997).

1. Make 18 photocopies each of the foundation patterns on page 29.

2. Cut out the photocopies on the outside line, which includes a ¼" seam allowance.

3. Set your stitch length to 12–15 stitches per inch.

4. With the printed side of the pattern up, position the flower-center foundation pattern over the wrong side of a floral print square. Pin the fabric in place through the marked side of the paper.

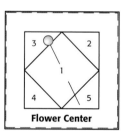

Flower Center

5. Place a 1¼" x 2" petal-fabric rectangle for piece 2 on top of piece 1, right sides together. Make sure the fabric extends beyond the sewing line for the seam allowance.

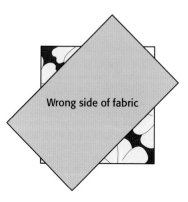

Wrong side of fabric

6. Hold the layers in place. Turn to the marked side. Sew on the line between areas 1 and 2, starting ¼" before the line and extending ¼" beyond.

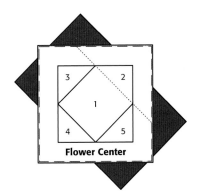

7. Fold the paper back on the seam line. Place a ruler along the edge of the paper and trim a ¼" seam allowance.

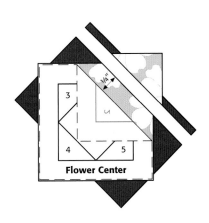

8. Press the seam out from the center square and trim excess fabric.

9. Continue adding pieces in numerical order until all the pieces have been sewn to the paper foundation.

10. Repeat the process to make the petal units using four petal foundation patterns per flower. Use a 1½" bright green print square to cover piece 1 and matching 1½" x 2" petal rectangles for pieces 2 and 3.

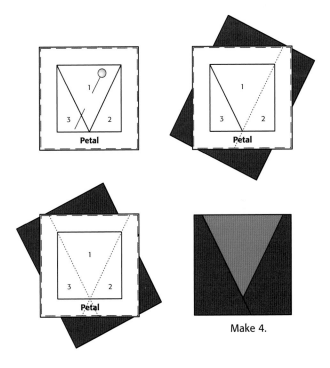

Make 4.

11. Trim the blocks to the outside cutting line and remove the paper before sewing the units together.

12. Sew a 1½" x 1½" bright green print square to each side of a petal unit. Press toward the green squares. Repeat.

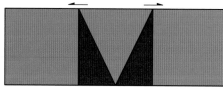

Make 2.

13. Sew two flower-petal units to opposite sides of a flower-center unit, orienting the petal points away from the center. Press toward the center unit.

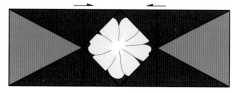

Make 1.

14. Sew the two petal rows from step 12 to the top and bottom of the center row from step 13, again orienting the petal points away from the center. Press seams away from the center row.

15. Repeat to make a total of 18 flower blocks: 3 red, 3 white, 2 orange, 2 light orange, 2 dark purple, 2 red-purple, 2 yellow, and 2 pink.

Assembling the Quilt

1. Referring to the quilt photo on page 24 and the illustration above right, arrange the blocks in diagonal rows. Sew the rows together, adding bright green print quarter-square triangles to the row ends as shown. Press seams in alternate directions from row to row.

2. Sew the bright green print half-square triangles to the corners of the quilt and press the seams toward the triangles.

Appliquéing the Leaves

1. Referring to "Needle-Turn Appliqué" on page 85, trace the leaf pattern on page 29. Prepare 82 leaves.

2. Position the leaves as shown in the quilt layout. Appliqué into place.

Adding the Borders

1. With right sides together, and stitching along the long edges, sew each ¾"-wide dark green strip to a 1½"-wide bright green print strip of the same length.

2. Sew each of the border units to the quilt top, following the directions for "Mitered Borders" on page 89.

Finishing Your Quilt

Refer to "General Directions," beginning on page 85, for specific directions regarding each of the following finishing steps.

1. Layer the quilt top with batting and backing; baste.

2. Machine or hand quilt as desired.

3. Trim the batting and backing even with the quilt-top edges.

4. Referring to "Traditional Binding" on page 93, prepare the 1¼" bright green print strips for binding and sew the binding to the quilt.

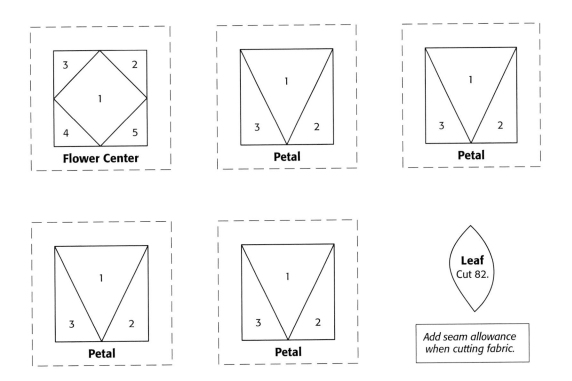

Wild Roses

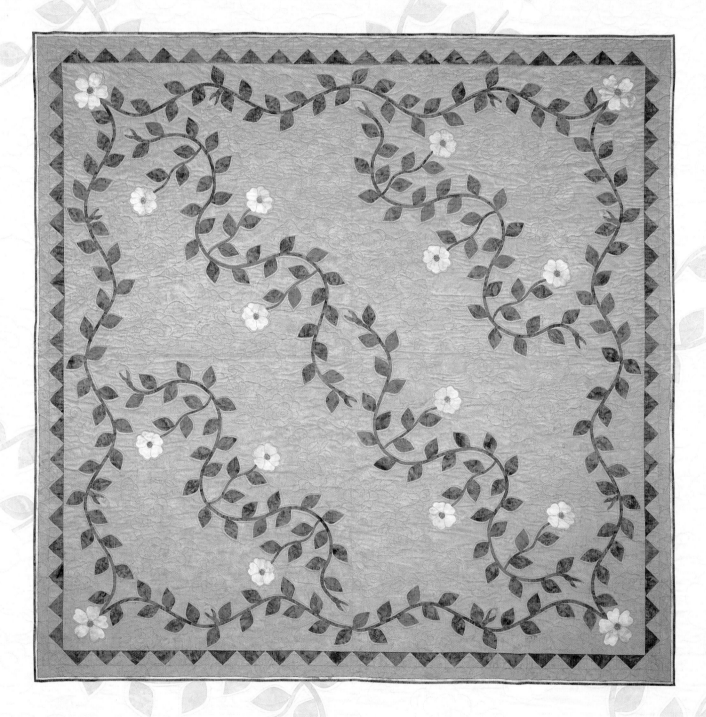

Finished Size: 88½" x 88½"

I could almost smell my favorite fragrance of wild roses
in bloom as I was appliquéing the roses on this quilt.
Their beautiful, delicate pink flowers surrounded
by fresh green leaves makes their appearance
just as delightful as their scent.

Materials

Yardages are based on 42"-wide fabric.

7 yards of light green for background and borders

4 yards of dark green for vines, leaves, rosebuds, flying geese, and binding

1 yard of light pink for roses and border accent

¼ yard of bright pink for rosebuds

⅛ yard of gold fabric for rose centers

8 yards of fabric for backing (pieced in 3 sections)

94" x 94" piece of batting

Embroidery floss in pink, gold, and yellow

24"-long ruler with a 45°-angle mark

Bias bars, ¼" and ⅜"

Freezer paper

Cutting

All measurements include ¼" seam allowances.

From the light green fabric, cut:
- 4 squares, 42" x 42"
- 7 strips, 2⅞" x 42"; crosscut into 80 squares, 2⅞" x 2⅞"
- 4 squares, 2½" x 2½"
- 9 strips, 2½" x 42"

From the dark green fabric, cut:
- 3 strips, 5¼" x 42"; crosscut into 20 squares, 5¼" x 5¼"
- 9 strips, 2" x 42"

From the light pink fabric, cut:
- 9 strips, 1¼" x 42"

Making Bias Strips for the Vines

1. With a single layer of dark green fabric on your rotary-cutting mat, place the 45°-angle line of a ruler parallel to the bottom edge. Cut away the corner of fabric and use this angled edge to measure and cut the necessary bias strips.

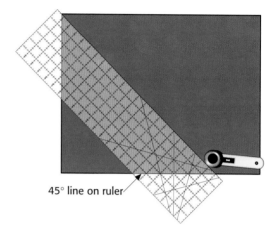

45° line on ruler

2. Cut enough 1⅛" strips to total a pieced length of 145".

3. Cut enough 1⅜" strips to total a pieced length of 600".

4. With right sides together, sew the 1⅛" strips together on the diagonal as shown to create a strip at least 145" long. Sew the 1⅜" strips together on the diagonal to create a strip at least 600" long.

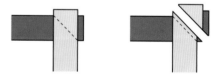

5. Cut the 1⅛" strip into 12 sections, 10½" long.

6. Cut the 1⅜" strip into eight sections, 42" long; two sections, 62" long; and two sections, 68" long.

7. Fold all of the sections in half lengthwise with wrong sides together. Press. Sew raw edges together with a ¼" seam.

8. Trim the seam allowance to ⅛" and slip the ¼" bias bar into the 10½" bias tubes. Adjust the seam so that it is centered on the bar. Steam press to flatten the tube, pressing the seam allowance to one side.

Bias bar

9. Repeat the procedure with the wider bias tubes using the ⅜" bias bar. Scoot the bias bar along inside the tubes and press as you go.

Appliqué Layout

1. With a water-soluble marking pen or pencil, mark a 40" square on each of the 42" light green fabric squares.

2. Pin two of the 42" bias vines in place on one of the four large background squares. From the drawn 40" line, mark the fabric at the indicated measurements for the vine placement. The numbers on the diagram indicate the number of inches in from the drawn line. Make gentle curves between these points with the vines. Baste one vine vertically, leaving ends raw. Baste the other vine horizontally, folding under the beginning raw end to cover the end of the vertical vine in the corner. Stop basting about 3" from the outside edges of the square and leave an extra 3" of the vine free. Repeat to make three more squares with vines.

3. Fold each of the four squares from step 2 in half in both directions and finger-press to mark the center of the squares.

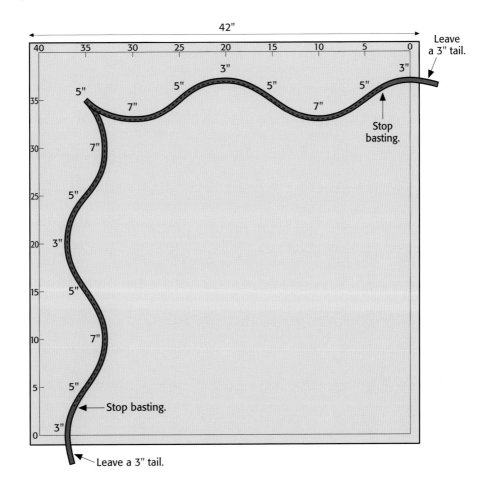

4. Take one of the 62" vines and place the middle of the vine so that it is oriented to the square as shown. Use a 10" or 11" round dinner plate to help shape the vines. Trim the ends of the vines if necessary. Baste in place. Make two.

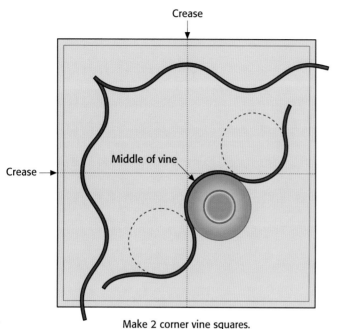

Make 2 corner vine squares.

5. Add a 10½" stem in the middle of each of the three curves. Place the strips in a gentle S curve and tuck the inner raw end of the stem under the main vine. Baste in place.

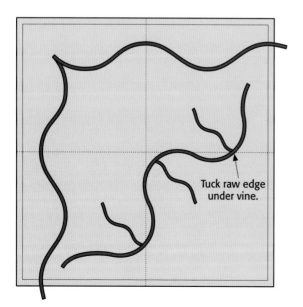

6. Pin one of the 68" vines in place to one of the remaining background squares, following the diagram. Use the round dinner plate to help shape the curves and add three of the 10½" stems to the center of each curve. Baste in place. Make 2.

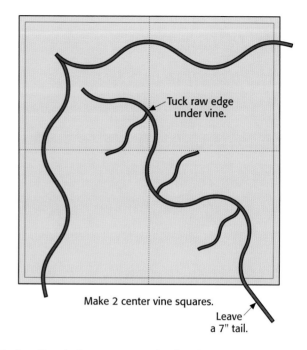

Make 2 center vine squares.

Leave a 7" tail.

7. Appliqué the vines to the background as described in "Invisible Machine Appliqué Stitch" on page 87 or "Hand Appliqué Stitch" on page 87.

Appliquéing the Leaves and Roses

1. Trace the pattern shapes on page 37, referring to the directions for freezer-paper or needle-turn appliqué on pages 85–86. Cut the required number of shapes from each appropriate fabric. Note that the roses are cut as one unit, with embroidery detailing being added for the petals later.

2. Refer to the quilt plan on page 36 for placement of leaves, roses, rose centers, and buds. Appliqué vines, leaves, roses, rose centers, and buds into place. Continue to leave ends of vines loose.

3. With two strands of pink floss, outline the rose petals using the stem stitch. Make French knots in and around the center of the flowers, using two strands of gold floss for half of the knots and two strands of yellow floss for the other half.

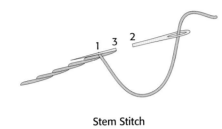

Stem Stitch

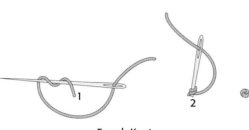

French Knot

Assembling the Quilt

1. Press and then trim each of the four quilt sections to measure 40½" x 40½". Pin the tail ends of the bias strips out of the way before cutting!

2. Sew the four square sections together with one of the corner vine squares placed in the bottom left corner and the other corner vine square placed in the top right corner. Place the remaining center vines squares in the opposing corners. Check quilt layout for proper placement. Press.

3. Pin the ends of the vines so that they meet at the middle of the outer edges of the quilt. To splice vines together, open the seam ½" on the end of one vine and tuck the raw end of the matching vine ½" inside. Trim inside vine, if necessary. Turn the end of the outer vine ¼" to the inside to create a

finished edge. Appliqué vines in place. Add leaves that go over the seam.

Add leaves that
go over the seams.

Splice vine.

4. Finish the center of the quilt by curving the ends of the vines into the next square and adding a rosebud and leaves to the end of each vine. Appliqué rosebuds and leaves into place.

Flying Geese Border

1. Using the 2⅞" squares of light green fabric and the 5¼" squares of dark green fabric, follow the directions on page 88 for "Quick and Easy Flying Geese" to make a total of 80 units.

2. Sew 20 of the flying-geese units end to end to make a pieced border. Press seams to one side. Make four borders.

3. Sew a border to both sides of the quilt top, placing the base of the dark green triangles toward the inside of the quilt. Press seams toward the quilt center.

4. Sew a 2½" light green square to each end of the two remaining borders. Press seams toward the squares. Sew these borders to the top and bottom of the quilt.

5. Referring to "Straight-Cut Borders" on page 89, add the 2½" light green borders.

Finishing Your Quilt

Refer to "General Directions," beginning on page 85, for specific directions regarding each of the following finishing steps.

1. Layer the quilt top with batting and backing; baste.

2. Machine or hand quilt as desired.

3. Trim the batting and backing even with the quilt-top edges.

4. For the pink border accent, sew the 1¼" light pink strips together end to end. Press seams open. Cut this strip into four sections, each measuring 89". Fold each section in half lengthwise with the wrong sides together and press. With the raw edges even and using a *scant* ¼" seam, sew the strips to each side of the quilt. Trim ends even with the quilt top.

5. Referring to "French Binding" on page 92, prepare the 2" dark green strips for binding and sew the binding to the quilt.

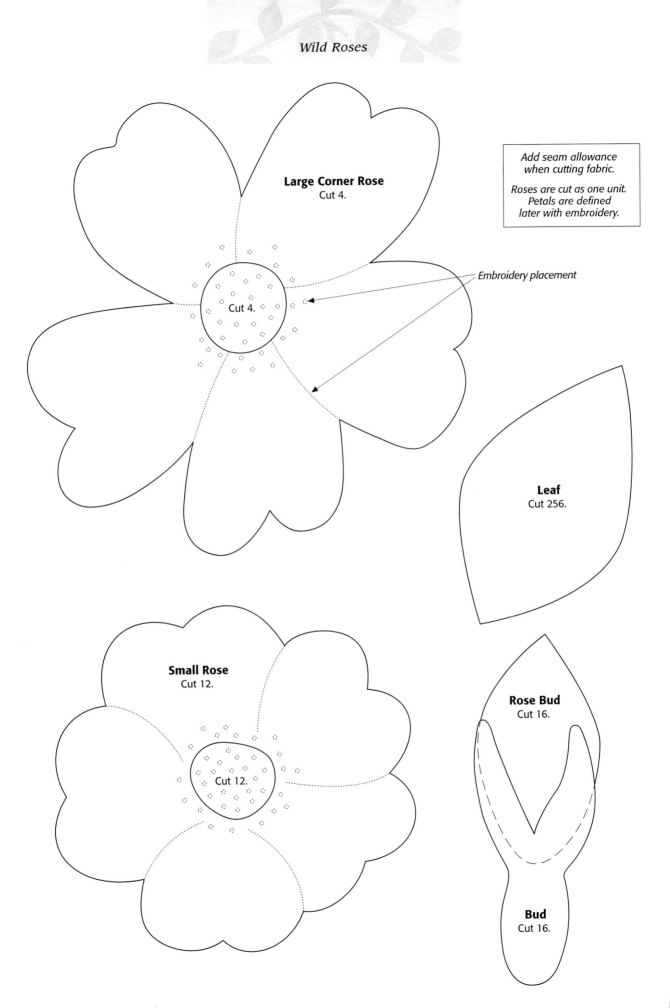

Large Corner Rose
Cut 4.

Cut 4.

*Add seam allowance
when cutting fabric.*

*Roses are cut as one unit.
Petals are defined
later with embroidery.*

Embroidery placement

Leaf
Cut 256.

Small Rose
Cut 12.

Cut 12.

Rose Bud
Cut 16.

Bud
Cut 16.

Riverbed

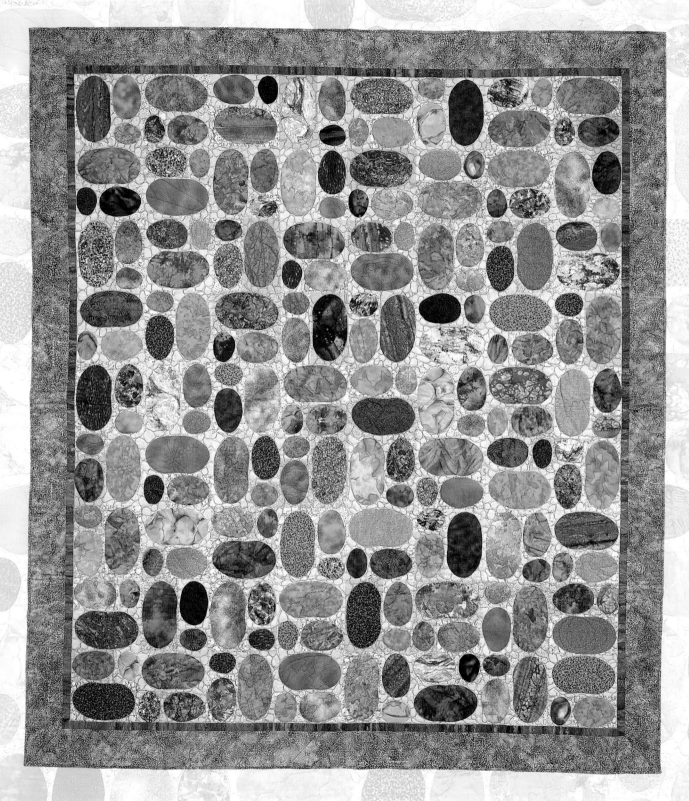

Finished Size: 83½" x 92½"
Finished Block Size: 9" x 9"

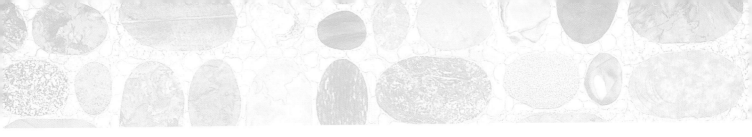

*I have always liked the worn, round shapes of river rocks
in their variety of earth tones. When I started collecting
fabrics with rock-like textures, I discovered it was
even more fun than collecting the rocks!*

Materials

Yardages are based on 42"-wide fabric.

6 yards of assorted light sand-colored fabrics for background

2¼ yards of light brown for outer border and binding

½ yard of medium brown for inner border

24 pieces, ¼ yard each, of stone fabric*

7½ yards of fabric for backing (3 widths, pieced horizontally)

89" x 98" piece of batting

Freezer paper

* *Selecting a big variety of stone fabrics will add to the interest of this quilt. Use your imagination when selecting fabric. Wood-grain textures, small prints, and batiks can make very realistic stones.*

Cutting

All measurements include ¼" seam allowance.

From assorted background fabrics, cut:

* 18 strips, 5½" x 42"; crosscut into 72 rectangles, 5½" x 9½"

* 8 strips, 3½" x 42"; crosscut into 72 rectangles, 3½" x 4½"

* 12 strips, 4½" x 42"; crosscut into 72 rectangles, 4½" x 6½"

From the medium brown fabric, cut:

* 8 strips, 1½" x 42"

From the light brown fabric, cut:

* 9 strips, 5" x 42"

* 10 strips, 2" x 42"

Making the Blocks

1. Sew the 3½" x 4½" rectangles to the 4½" x 6½" rectangles along the 4½" edges. Press seam allowances in either direction.

2. Sew the pieced rectangles from step 1 to the 5½" x 9½" rectangles as shown. Press seam allowances toward the large rectangle.

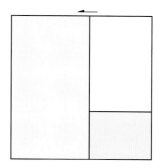

Make 72.

3. Using the assorted stone fabrics, refer to "Invisible Machine Appliqué" on page 86 for details on preparing the stone appliqués.

4. Pin three stone appliqués on each of the blocks and machine appliqué in place.

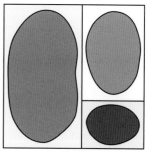

Make 72.

Assembling the Quilt Top

1. Sew eight blocks into a horizontal row. Randomly turn the blocks to avoid the look of a planned garden path. Make nine rows. Press the seams in opposite directions from row to row.

2. Sew the rows together. Press all seam allowances in the same direction.

3. Sew the inner-border strips together end to end. Cut to make two strips that are 85" long and two that are 94" long. Repeat with the outer-border strips.

4. Sew the inner-border strips to the outer-border strips. Press seams toward the outer border.

5. Referring to "Mitered Borders" on page 89, sew the borders to the quilt top and miter the corners.

Finishing Your Quilt

Refer to "General Directions," beginning on page 85, for specific directions in each of the following finishing steps.

1. Layer the quilt top with batting and backing; baste.

2. Hand or machine quilt as desired.

3. Trim the batting and backing even with the quilt-top edges.

4. Referring to "French Binding" on page 92, prepare the 2" light brown strips for binding and sew the binding to the quilt.

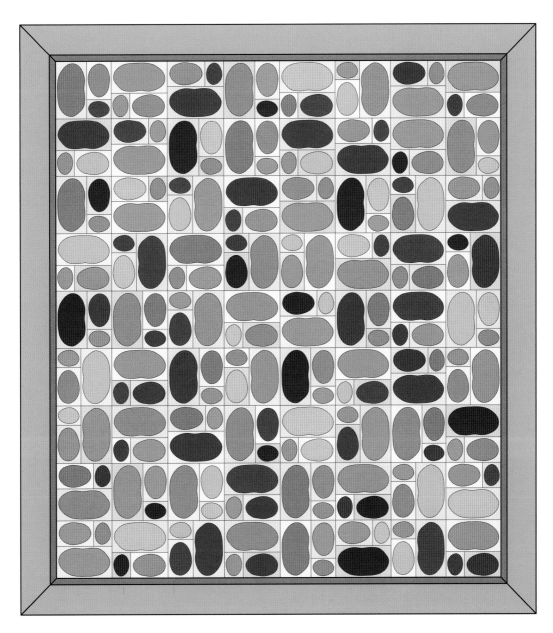

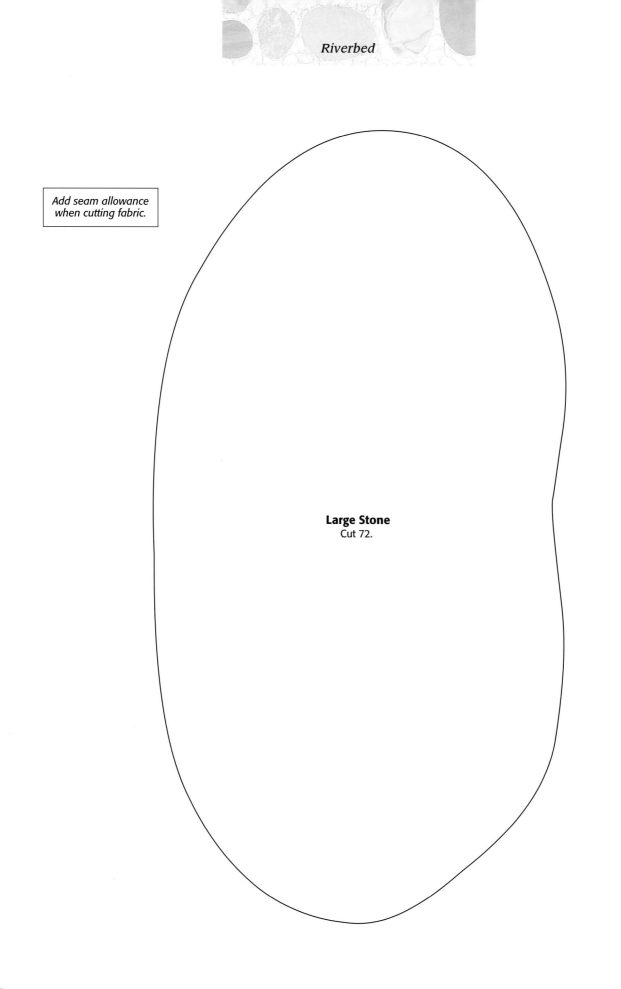

Add seam allowance
when cutting fabric.

Large Stone
Cut 72.

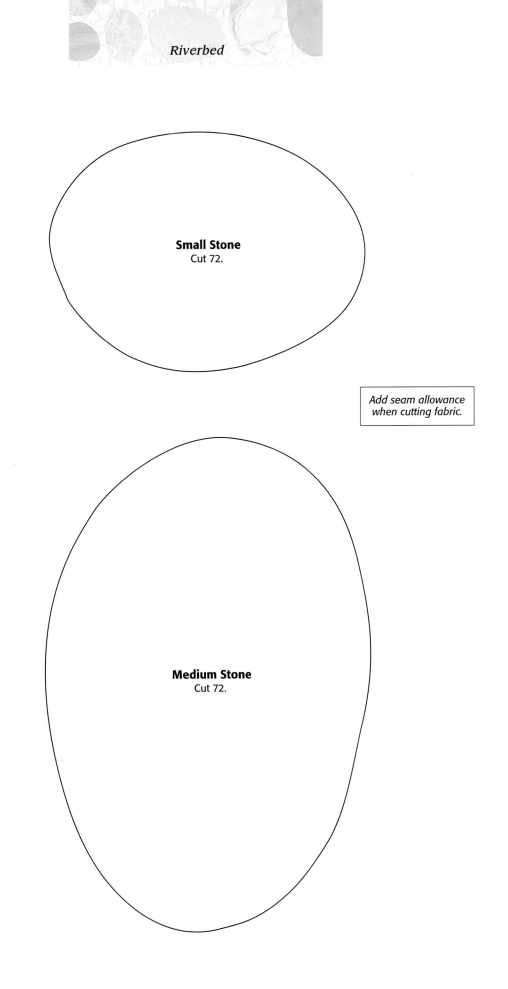

Small Stone
Cut 72.

Add seam allowance
when cutting fabric.

Medium Stone
Cut 72.

Sticks and Stones

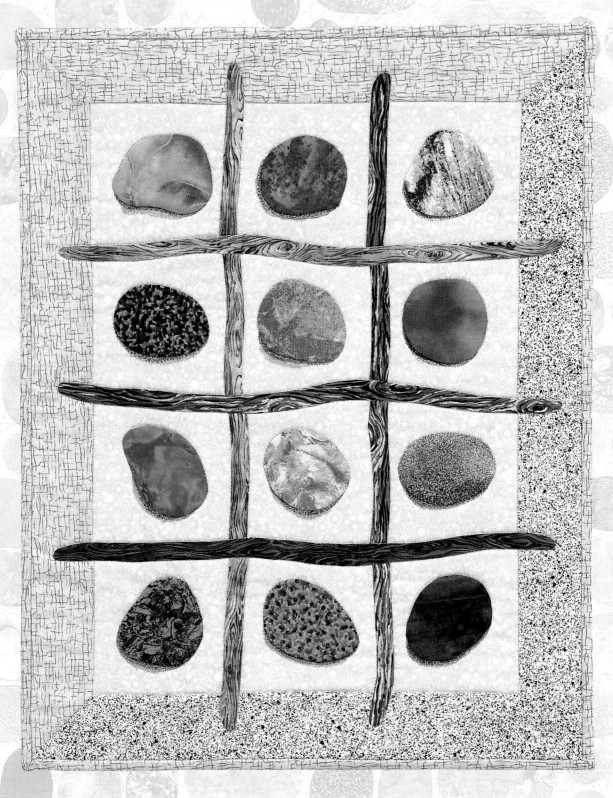

Finished Size: 18" x 22½"

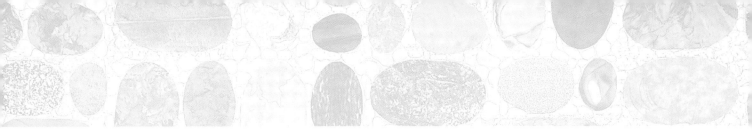

This simple little wall hanging is the perfect gift for any rock hound, or, if the lucky recipient isn't a stone collector, you can make it in prints of his or her favorite colors.

Materials

Yardages are based on 42"-wide fabric.

½ yard of light gray for the two lighter sides of the border and binding

¼ yard of medium gray for the two darker sides of the border

1 fat quarter of sand-colored fabric for background

⅛ yard each of 2–3 wood-textured fabrics for sticks

12 assorted 4" squares of stone fabric

¼ yard of black tulle

⅔ yard of fabric for backing

22" x 26" piece of batting

Black fine-tip permanent marker

Freezer paper

Cutting

All measurements include ¼" seam allowances.

From the background fabric, cut:
• 1 rectangle, 14" x 18½"

From the lighter border fabric, cut:
• 2 strips, 2½" x 42"; crosscut into 1 strip, 2½" x 19", and 1 strip, 2½" x 24"
• 3 strips, 2" x 42"

From the darker border fabric, cut:
• 2 strips, 2½" x 42"; crosscut into 1 strip, 2½" x 19", and 1 strip, 2½" x 24"

Making the Background

1. Referring to "Mitered Borders" on page 89, sew the lighter border strips to the top and left side of the 14" x 18½" background rectangle and the darker border strips to the bottom and right side of the rectangle.

2. With a pencil, lightly mark a 4½" grid on the background rectangle as shown.

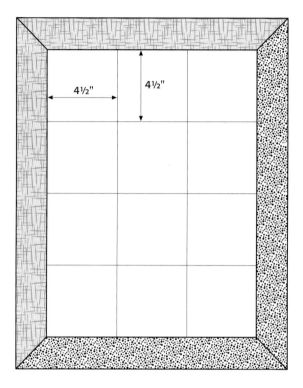

Appliquéing the Sticks and Stones

1. Trace and cut the pattern shapes on pages 48–51 as directed for "Freezer-Paper Appliqué" on page 85.

2. First appliqué the longer sticks, centering them over the vertical pencil lines on the background rectangle. Then place the shorter sticks over the horizontal pencil lines. Turn the middle stick in the opposite direction to keep the grid from looking too precise.

3. Pin the stones to the background, matching their numbers for proper placement.

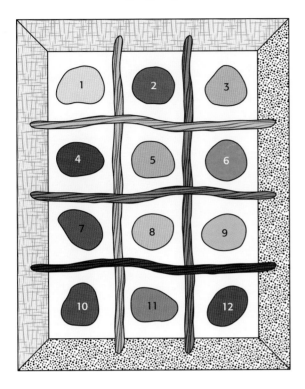

4. Before appliquéing the stones, cut a small piece of tulle about ½" wide to match the bottom left curve of each stone. Slip this piece under the stone before appliquéing so that just ¼" shows. This will add dimension to the stone. Use the permanent marker to make tiny little dots on the tulle, creating the impression of a shadow gradually darkening toward the edge of the stone.

5. Appliqué the stones, leaving the edges of the tulle loose.

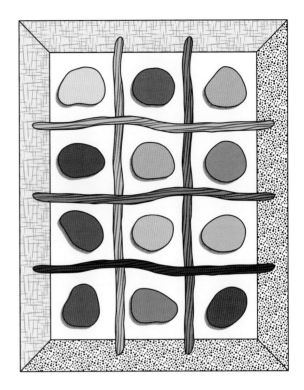

Finishing Your Quilt

Refer to "General Directions," beginning on page 85, for specific directions regarding each of the following finishing steps.

1. Layer the quilt top with batting and backing; baste.

2. Machine or hand quilt as desired.

3. Trim the batting and backing even with the quilt-top edges.

4. Referring to "French Binding" on page 92, prepare the 2" light gray strips for binding and sew the binding to the quilt.

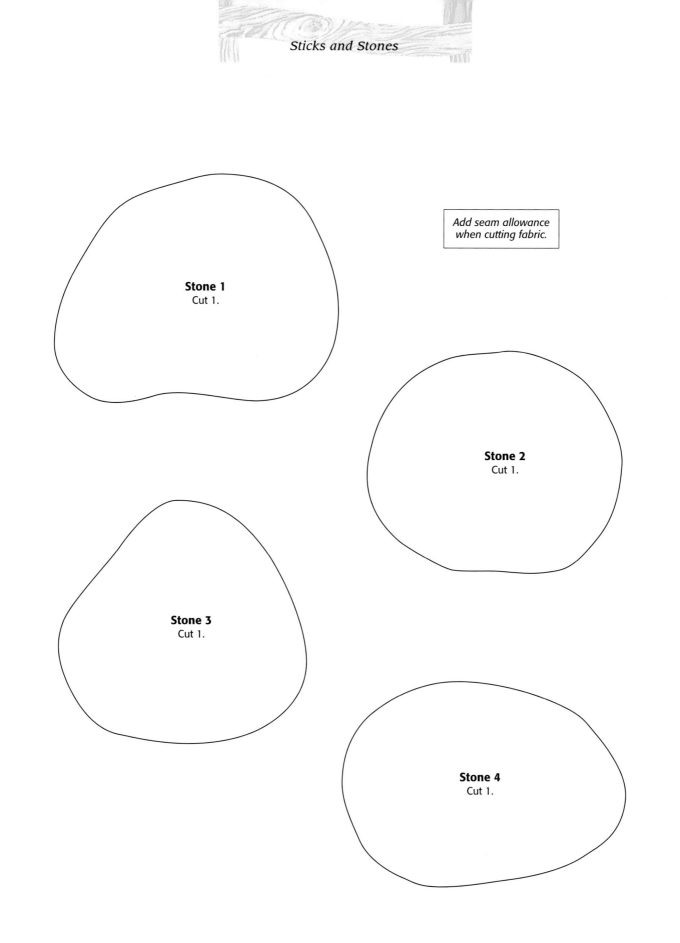

Stone 1
Cut 1.

Add seam allowance
when cutting fabric.

Stone 2
Cut 1.

Stone 3
Cut 1.

Stone 4
Cut 1.

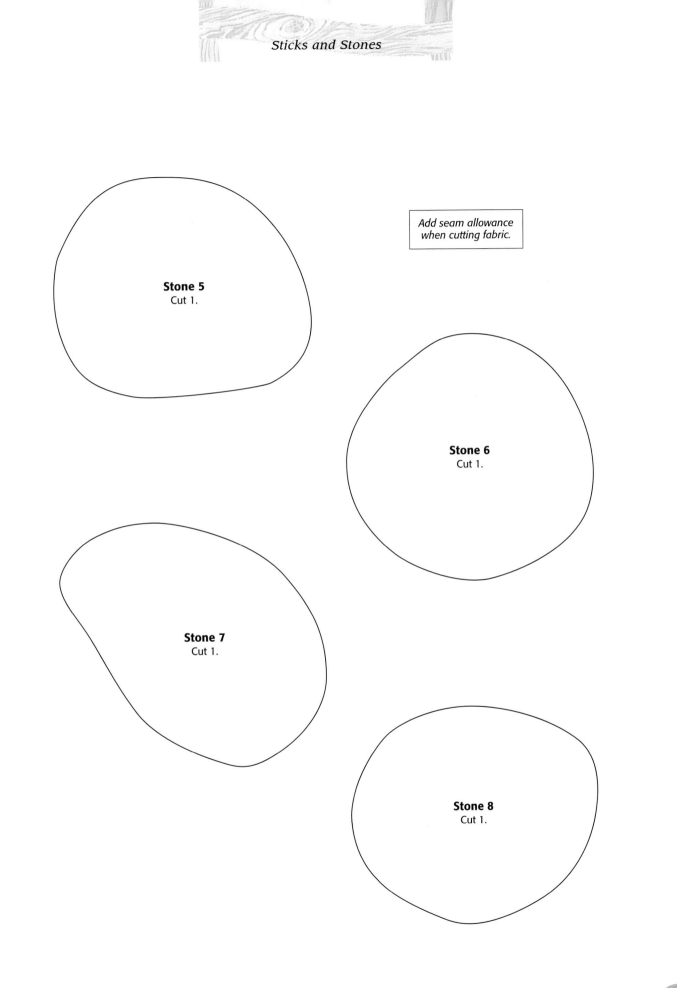

Add seam allowance
when cutting fabric.

Stone 5
Cut 1.

Stone 6
Cut 1.

Stone 7
Cut 1.

Stone 8
Cut 1.

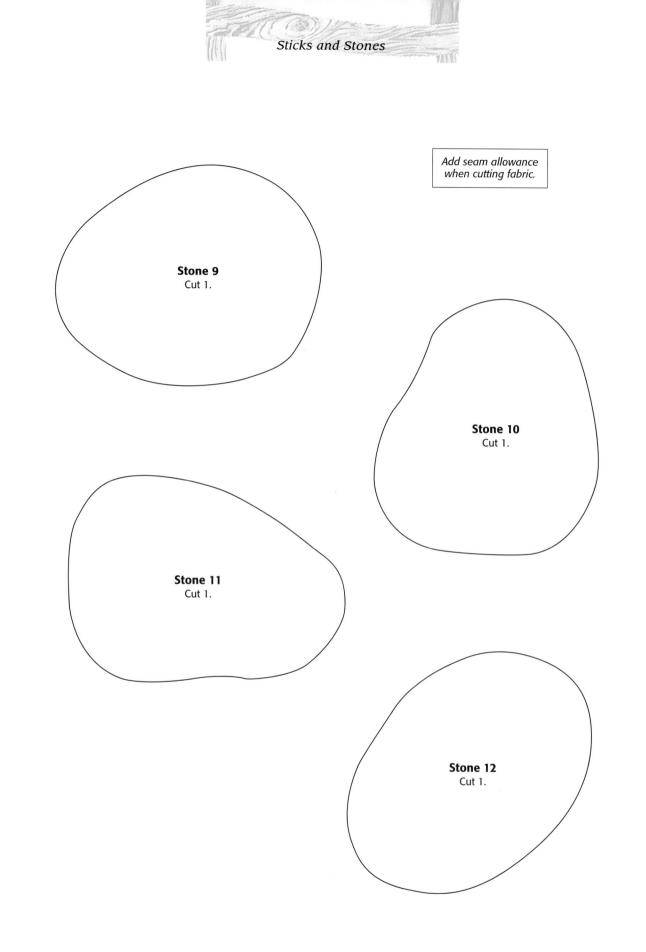

Add seam allowance
when cutting fabric.

Stone 9
Cut 1.

Stone 10
Cut 1.

Stone 11
Cut 1.

Stone 12
Cut 1.

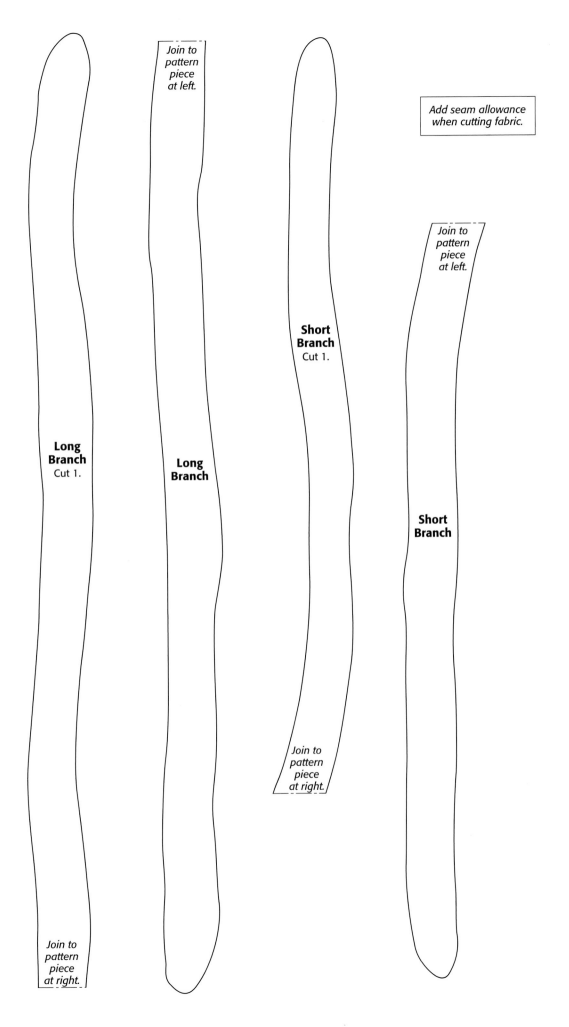

*Join to
pattern
piece
at left.*

*Add seam allowance
when cutting fabric.*

*Join to
pattern
piece
at left.*

**Short
Branch**
Cut 1.

**Long
Branch**
Cut 1.

**Long
Branch**

**Short
Branch**

*Join to
pattern
piece
at right.*

*Join to
pattern
piece
at right.*

Through the Forest

Finished Size: 66½" x 80½"

*At one delightful spot on my walk, if I am very quiet
and pick just the right time of day, I may spot a deer,
an owl, a rabbit, or other woodland creatures.
You'll find them all hidden in this quilt!*

Materials

Yardages are based on 42"-wide fabric.

2⅝ yards of tan for background

1¾ yards of brown print for outer border and binding

¾ yard total of assorted brown prints for tree trunks

½ yard of green print for inner border

21 fat eighths of tree prints

Assortment of scraps for animal appliqués

4½ yards of fabric for backing (pieced horizontally)

71" x 85" piece of batting

Embroidery floss in black, brown, cream, and white

Freezer paper

Cutting

All measurements include ¼" seam allowances.

From the tan background fabric, cut:
- 17 strips, 3⅞" x 42"; crosscut into 168 squares, 3⅞" x 3⅞"
- 2 strips, 1½" x 42"; crosscut into 7 pieces, 1½" x 6½"
- 2 strips, 1" x 42"; crosscut into 12 pieces, 1" x 6½"
- 2 strips 3½" x 42"; crosscut into 10 rectangles, 3½" x 6½", and 2 rectangles, 3½" x 4½"
- 2 strips, 4½" x 42"; crosscut into 7 rectangles, 4½" x 6½"

From each of the 21 fat eighths of tree prints, cut:
- 2 squares, 7¼" x 7¼", for a total of 42 squares

From the assorted brown prints, cut:
- 75 pieces, 1½" x 6½"
- 8 pieces, 1½" x 4½"

From the green inner-border print, cut:
- 8 strips, 1½" x 42"

From the brown outer-border print, cut:
- 8 strips, 4½" x 42"
- 8 strips, 2" x 42"

Making the Tree Blocks

1. Using the 168 background squares and the 42 tree-print squares, follow the directions for "Quick and Easy Flying Geese" on page 88.

2. Pair matching tree-print units from step 1 and sew into sets of two along the length of the rectangles. Press seams toward the bottom units.

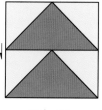

Make 83.

3. To the right of seven tree blocks, sew a 1½" x 6½" background piece. Press toward the strips.

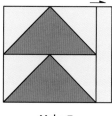

Make 7.

4. To the right of 70 tree blocks, sew a 1½" x 6½" tree-trunk piece. Press toward the strips.

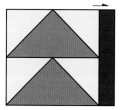

Make 70.

Assembling the Rows

1. To make the top row, sew the seven blocks from step 3 of "Making the Tree Blocks" together into a horizontal row. Press toward the background strips. To the left end of the row, sew a 1" x 6½" background piece. Press. To the right end of the row, sew a tree block from step 2 of "Making the Tree Block" and a 1" x 6½" background piece. Press seam toward the background piece.

Top Row

2. Sew seven blocks from step 4 of "Making the Tree Blocks" together into a horizontal row. Press seams toward the tree-trunk pieces. To the left end of the row, sew a 3½" x 6½" background rectangle and a 1½" x 6½" tree-trunk piece. Press seams toward the rectangles. To the right end of the row, sew a 3½" x 6½" background rectangle. Press the seam toward the rectangle. Repeat to make five rows.

Make 5 rows.

3. Sew seven blocks from step 4 of "Making the Tree Blocks" together into a horizontal row. Press seams toward the tree-trunk pieces. To the left end of the row, sew a 1" x 6½" background piece. Press the seam toward the background piece. To the right end of the row, sew a tree block from step 2 and a 1" x 6½" background strip. Press seams toward the strips. Repeat to make five rows.

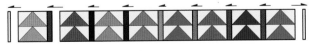

Make 5 rows.

4. To make the bottom row, sew a 1½" x 4½" tree-trunk piece to a 4½" x 6½" background rectangle. Press toward the tree-trunk piece. Repeat to make seven blocks. Sew these blocks into a horizontal row. Press toward the tree-trunk pieces. To the left end of the row, sew a 3½" x 4½" background rectangle and a 1½" x 4½" tree-trunk piece. Press seams toward the tree-trunk piece. To the right end of the row, sew a 3½" x 4½" background rectangle. Press the seam toward the tree-trunk piece.

Make 7.

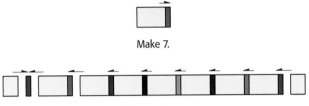

Bottom Row

5. Referring to the quilt plan, sew the rows together. Begin with the top row, then alternate rows from steps 2 and 3 of this section, and end with the bottom row. Press all seam allowances in the same direction.

Adding the Border

Referring to "Straight-Cut Borders" on page 89, add the 1½" green print strips for the inner border and the 4½" brown print strips for the outer border.

Adding the Appliqué

1. Trace and cut the pattern shapes on page 57, referring to the directions for freezer-paper or needle-turn appliqué on pages 85–86. Due to the size of the designs, add only 1/16" seam allowance to each one to reduce bulk.

2. Referring to the quilt plan on page 56 for placement, appliqué each design into place.

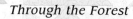

3. Sew details on animals using one strand of floss. Using brown or black floss, outline shapes with a stem stitch. Make the animal's eyes with French knots. Use a satin stitch for the rabbit's tail.

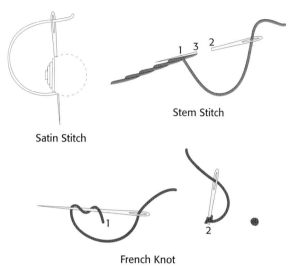

Satin Stitch

Stem Stitch

French Knot

Finishing Your Quilt

Refer to "General Directions," beginning on page 85, for specific directions regarding each of the following finishing steps.

1. Layer the quilt top with batting and backing; baste.

2. Machine or hand quilt as desired.

3. Trim the batting and backing even with the quilt-top edges.

4. Referring to "French Binding" on page 92, prepare the 2" brown print strips for binding and sew the binding to the quilt.

Embroidery
placement

Add seam allowance
when cutting fabric.

Autumn Afternoon

Finished Size: 61½" x 74½"

*My favorite time of year is autumn with its golden glow,
especially during the soft shadows of the afternoon.
Capture the beautiful shades of fall with a warm
array of batik prints, and add an accent of
purple for a finishing touch.*

Materials

Yardages are based on 42"-wide fabric.

⅝ yard of purple for inner border

24 fat quarters of assorted batik prints in warm shades of orange, yellow, pink, purple, beige, and brown for rows and outer border

4 yards of fabric for backing (pieced horizontally)

½ yard of batik print for binding

66" x 79" piece of batting

Bias Square ruler or any ruler with a 45°-angle mark

Cutting

All measurements include ¼" seam allowances.

From the batik prints, cut:
- 3 strips, 3½" x 21", from each of the 24 batik prints; crosscut into varying lengths from 9" to 21"

- 18 strips, 4½" x 21"

From the inner-border fabric, cut:
- 8 strips, 2" x 42"

From the binding fabric, cut:
- 8 strips, 2" x 42"

Cutting and Arranging the Strips

1. Cut one horizontal row at a time. To cut two adjoining pieces, stack two 3½"-wide rectangles together with right sides up. Align the 45° line of the ruler along the edge of the strips. Cut a 45° angle on the right end of the rectangles. Turn the top rectangle around so that the angles match up. Place another rectangle on top of the last rectangle cut and repeat until you have a row of either four or five rectangles that measures at least 54". Vary the direction of the diagonal cuts by placing the 45° line of the ruler on the top or bottom fabric edge.

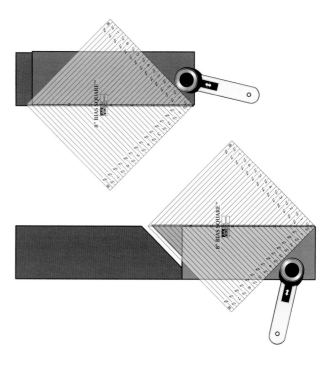

2. Place the rows on your design wall or floor to check the color placement and angles. Begin with four pieces in the first row and five in the second row; continue to alternate. Arrange 21 rows.

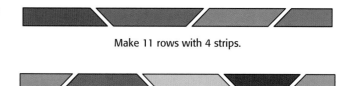

Make 11 rows with 4 strips.

Make 10 rows with 5 strips.

Sewing the Pieces into Rows

1. With right sides together, sew pieces together in each row, offsetting the ends of each piece to allow for an accurate ¼" seam allowance. Press the seam allowances to one side.

2. Trim each row to measure 50½".

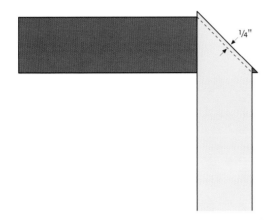

3. Sew the rows together, alternating stitching direction from row to row to help prevent wavy rows. Press all seam allowances in the same direction. Sew the rows into seven-row sections, and then sew these sections together.

Piecing the Borders

1. Use the 4½" x 21" strips to make the top and bottom borders. Using the same technique that you used for the interior of the quilt, cut four strips at 45° angles. Vary the direction of the angles, and also vary the strip lengths from 12" to 20". Sew these strips together. Cut to make a border that measures 63". Press seam allowances to one side. Repeat to make a second strip.

2. Use the remaining 4½" x 21" strips to make the side borders. Using the same technique as for the top and bottom borders, cut five strips at 45° angles. Vary the direction of the angles, and also vary the strip lengths from 12" to 20". Sew these strips together. Cut to make a border that measures 76". Press seam allowances to one side. Repeat to make a second strip.

3. Sew the 2" inner-border strips together into pairs. Press. Cut two strips to measure 63" and two to measure 76".

4. Sew the 63" and 76" inner-border strips to pieced border strips of the same length. Press toward the inner-border strips.

5. Referring to "Mitered Borders" on page 89, sew the borders to the quilt top.

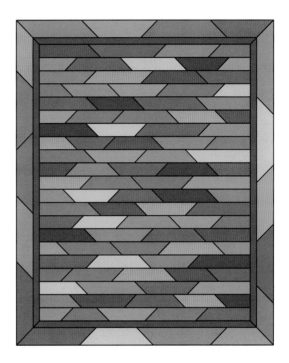

Finishing Your Quilt

Refer to "General Directions," beginning on page 85, for specific directions regarding each of the following finishing steps.

1. Layer the quilt top with batting and backing; baste.

2. Machine or hand quilt as desired.

3. Trim the batting and backing even with the quilt-top edges.

4. Referring to "French Binding" on page 92, prepare the 2" batik strips for binding and sew the binding to the quilt.

Winter Morning

Finished Size: 61½" x 74½"

 A walk on a cold winter morning inspired me to make this
toasty-warm wool quilt. I used the cool gray palette of
January to pick the colors and added wool batting
and a soft cotton backing to make this quilt
a real treat on a chilly winter night.

Materials

Most of the fabric used in this quilt came from recycled wool. I collected wool clothing from thrift stores and used my husband's outdated wool suits. The fabrics are mostly 100% wool with a couple that contain a low-polyester blend. If you are making this quilt from new wool, use the yardage requirements listed for "Autumn Afternoon" on page 60.

8–9 wool garments of suiting wool for rows and outer border

⅝ yard of dark wool for inner border, or a leg from 1 pair of pants (that will also be enough for a traditional binding)

⅝ yard of dark wool for binding, or the other leg from pants used for inner border

4 yards of cotton fabric for backing (pieced horizontally)

66" x 79" piece of batting

Bias Square ruler or any ruler with a 45°-angle mark

Preparing the Fabric

Machine wash the garments in warm water with a mild soap recommended for wool. Dry in the dryer on a low heat setting. If a garment becomes felted, save it for another project. Cut apart garments at their seams, cutting off waistbands, zippers, and buttons.

Cutting

From the wool fabric, cut:

- 18 strips, 4½" x approximately 21" for border

- Cut the rest of the wool into 3½"-wide strips in varying lengths from 9" to 20".

From the inner-border fabric, cut:

- 8 strips, 2" x 42", or cut one pant leg into 2" strips

From the binding fabric, cut:

- 8 strips, 1½" x 42", or cut one pant leg into 1½" strips for a total length of 300"

Cutting and Arranging the Strips

1. Cut one horizontal row at a time. To cut two adjoining pieces, stack two 3½"-wide rectangles together with right sides up. Align the 45° line of the ruler along the edge of the strips. Cut a 45° angle on the right end of the rectangles. Turn the top rectangle around so that the angles match up. Place another rectangle on top of the last rectangle cut and repeat until you have a row of either four or five rectangles that measures at least 54". Vary the direction of the diagonal cuts by placing the 45° line of the ruler on the top or bottom fabric edge.

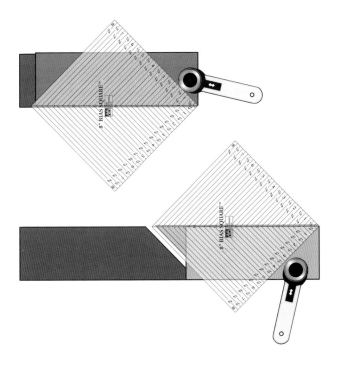

2. Place the rows on your design wall or floor to check the color placement and angles. Begin with four pieces in the first row and five in the second row; continue to alternate. Arrange 21 rows.

Make 11 rows with 4 strips.

Make 10 rows with 5 strips.

Sewing the Pieces into Rows

1. With right sides together, sew pieces together in each row, offsetting the ends of each piece to allow for an accurate ¼" seam allowance. Press the seam allowances to one side.

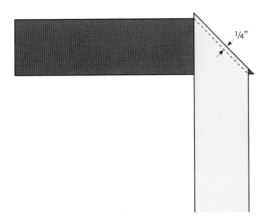

2. Trim each row to measure 50½".

3. Sew the rows together, alternating stitching direction from row to row to help prevent wavy rows. Press all seam allowances in the same direction. Sew the rows into seven-row sections, and then sew these sections together.

Piecing the Borders

1. Use the 4½" x 21" strips to make the top and bottom borders. Using the same technique that you used for the interior of the quilt, cut four strips at 45° angles. Vary the direction of the angles, and also vary the strip lengths from 12" to 20". Sew these strips together. Cut to make a border that measures 63". Press seam allowances to one side. Repeat to make a second strip.

2. Use the remaining 4½" x 21" strips to make the side borders. Using the same technique as for the top and bottom borders, cut five strips at 45° angles. Vary the direction of the angles, and also vary the strip lengths from 12" to 20". Sew these strips together. Cut to make a border that measures 76". Press seam allowances to one side. Repeat to make a second strip.

3. Sew the 2" inner-border strips together into pairs. Press. Cut two strips to measure 63" and two to measure 76".

4. Sew the 63" and 76" inner-border strips to pieced border strips of the same length. Press toward the inner-border strips.

5. Referring to "Mitered Borders" on page 89, sew the borders to the quilt top.

Finishing Your Quilt

Refer to "General Directions," beginning on page 85, for specific directions regarding each of the following finishing steps.

1. Layer the quilt top with batting and backing; baste.

2. Machine or hand quilt as desired.

3. Trim the batting and backing even with the quilt-top edges.

4. Referring to "Traditional Binding" on page 93, prepare the 1½" wool strips for binding and sew the binding to the quilt.

Wool Pillow

Finished Size: 18" x 18"

To make curling up by a winter fire even cozier, stitch up this wool pillow as a companion to your "Winter Morning" wool quilt. Attractive as well as comfy, it will provide an excellent winter accent to your living room decor.

Materials

8 coordinating 3½"-wide wool strips for pillow top (one gray-blue fabric, various shades of gray and brown fabrics in solids, small plaids, and her-ringbone prints)*

¼ yard of charcoal wool for border

⅝ yard of gray wool for backing

20" x 20" piece of muslin

20" x 20" piece of batting

Bias Square ruler or any ruler with a 45°-angle mark

18" pillow form

Basting spray (optional)

* *If using recycled wool, follow the instructions on page 64 for "Preparing the Fabric."*

Cutting

From the 8 wool strips, cut a total of:

- 2 strips, 3½" x 15½"

- 6 strips, 3½" x 12½"

From the charcoal wool, cut:

- 4 strips, 2" x 20"

From the gray wool, cut:

- 2 pieces, 13½" x 18½"

Sewing the Strips

1. Layer two 3½" x 12½" strips together with right sides up. On the right end of the layered strips, align the 45° line of the ruler along the top edge. Cut along the edge of the ruler. Turn the bottom rectangle around so that the angles match. Repeat to make two sets.

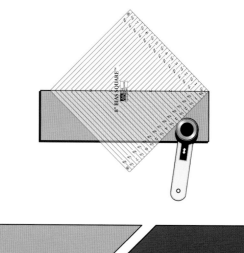

Make 2.

2. Layer two 3½" x 12½" strips together with right sides up. On the right end of the layered strips, align the 45° line of the ruler along the bottom edge. Cut along the edge of the ruler. Turn the bottom rectangle around so that the angles match. Make one.

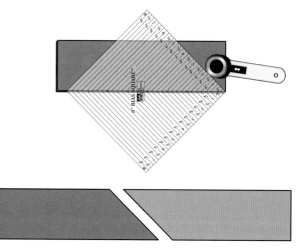

Make 1.

3. With right sides together, sew the angled ends of the strip sets together, offsetting the points to allow for an accurate ¼" seam. Be careful not to stretch the bias as you sew. Press the seam allowances open.

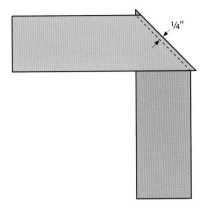

4. Trim each of the three strip sets to measure 15½". Trim either or both sides to vary the location of the angle.

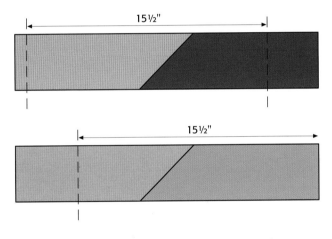

5. Sew the 3½" x 15½" strips between the pieced strip sets along the long edges. Press toward the solid strips.

6. Referring to "Mitered Borders" on page 89, use the 2" charcoal strips to sew a border to the pillow top.

Quilting the Pillow Top

1. Layer the muslin, batting, and pillow top. Baste, pin baste, or use basting spray to hold the layers together.

2. Machine or hand quilt. This pillow was first machine quilted in the ditch and then free-motion quilted using wood-grain designs.

3. Trim excess batting and muslin so that the pillow measures 18½".

Making the Pillow Back

1. On each 13½" x 18½" backing piece, turn ¼" under on one of the 13½" edges and press. Turn under again by 1"; press and edgestitch close to the inner fold.

2. Place the backing pieces right sides together with the pillow top, overlapping the stitched edges of the backing pieces and keeping the raw edges even. Pin all sides, and then stitch completely around the pillow with a ¼" seam. Clip corners at an angle to reduce bulk, being careful to leave at least ¼" from each stitched corner.

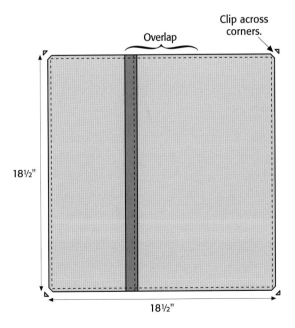

3. Turn the completed pillow cover right side out and press. Insert the pillow form.

The Seasons

Finished Size: 56½" x 72½"

*Northern Idaho enjoys the beauty of all four seasons;
they are just a little unevenly divided! The winter season
can last up to five months... making the spring all
the more welcome and spectacular.*

Materials

Yardages are based on 42"-wide fabric.

1⅜ yards of brown print for outer border and binding

⅝ yard total of fence fabrics

½ yard of tree background fabric for each of the 4 seasons*

⅜ yard of mountain fabric for each of the 4 seasons

⅜ yard of field fabric for each of the 4 seasons

⅜ yard of green print for inner border

¼ yard of sky fabric for each of the 4 seasons

¼ yard of tree fabric for each of the 4 seasons**

⅛ yard of tree-trunk fabric, or a variety of scraps

3⅝ yards of fabric for backing (pieced horizontally)

61" x 77" piece of batting

Ruler with a 30°-angle line

* *In two of the seasons I used the same fabric for the mountains and the tree backgrounds. If you would like to do the same, you will need ⅝ yard.*

** *You might want to use a variety of green prints for the trees within each season. A 5¼" square will make two tree blocks.*

Cutting

All measurements include ¼" seam allowances.

From each of the sky fabrics, cut:
- 3 strips, 2½" x 42"; crosscut into 8 rectangles, 2½" x 5⅞". Remaining strip pieces will be used in the construction of the mountain-and-sky row.

From each of the mountain fabrics, cut:
- 3 strips, 2½" x 42"; crosscut into 4 rectangles, 2½" x 11¾". Remaining strip pieces will be used in the construction of the mountain-and-sky row.

From each of the tree fabrics, cut:
- 1 strip, 5¼" x 42"; crosscut into 5 squares, 5¼" x 5¼"

From each of the tree background fabrics, cut:
- 2 strips, 2⅞" x 42"; crosscut into 20 squares, 2⅞" x 2⅞"
- 3 strips, 2½" x 42"; crosscut into 6 rectangles, 2½" x 6½", and 18 rectangles, 2½" x 2¼"

From the tree-trunk fabric, cut:
- 1 strip, 2½" x 42"; crosscut into 36 rectangles, 1" x 2½"

From each of the field fabrics, cut:
- 2 strips, 1½" x 42"
- 2 strips, 1¼" x 42"; crosscut into 3 strips, 1¼" x 21"
- 3 strips, 1⅛" x 42"; crosscut into 6 strips, 1⅛" x 21"

From the fence fabric, cut:
- 12 strips, 1" x 42"; crosscut into 24 strips, 1" x 21"
- 4 strips, 1¼" x 42"; crosscut into 44 rectangles, 1¼" x 3½"

From the green inner-border fabric, cut:
- 7 strips, 1½" x 42"

From the brown outer-border fabric, cut:
- 7 strips, 3½" x 42"
- 7 strips, 2" x 42"

NOTE: Make one seasonal panel at a time. Each panel is made up of three pieced rows: a mountain-and-sky row, a tree row, and a fence row.

Making One Mountain-and-Sky Row

1. Stack two 2½" x 5⅞" sky rectangles with wrong sides together. Placing the 30° line of the ruler on the right end of the strips, cut along the edge of the ruler as shown. Stack and cut a total of four pairs.

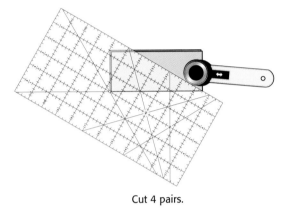

Cut 4 pairs.

2. Fold a 2½" x 11¾" mountain rectangle in half with wrong sides together. Place the fold to the left side and cut a 30° angle from the right side as shown. Cut four.

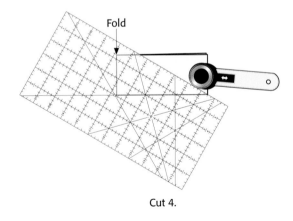

Cut 4.

3. Open the folded mountain pieces. Sew the angled end of a sky piece to each angled side of a mountain piece, offsetting the points of each piece to allow for an accurate ¼" seam.

Press seams toward the mountain pieces. Trim units evenly on both sides to measure 12½".

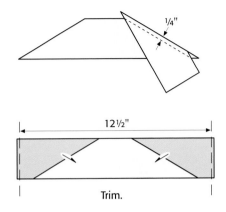

Trim.

4. Sew the mountain units together into a horizontal row. Press seams in either direction. Press all seam allowances in the same direction.

5. Piece two sky strips together. Cut to measure 48½". Press. Sew this strip to the top of the pieced mountain-and-sky row. Press the seam toward the sky strip.

6. Piece two mountain strips together. Cut to measure 48½". Sew this strip to the bottom of the section from step 5. Press the seam toward the mountain strip.

Making One Tree Row

1. Follow the directions on page 88 for "Quick and Easy Flying Geese," using the 5¼" squares of tree fabric and the 2⅞" squares of tree background fabric. This will make 20 flying-geese units, each measuring 2½" x 4½".

2. Pair matching flying-geese units from step 1 and sew into sets of two along the length of the rectangles. Press toward the bottom units. Make nine.

Make 9.

3. Sew a 2¼" x 2½" tree background piece to opposite sides of a 1" x 2½" tree-trunk rectangle, stitching along the 2½" edges. Press toward the tree trunk. Make nine.

Make 9.

4. Sew a tree-trunk unit to the bottom of each tree unit from step 2.

5. Sew six tree units together in pairs to make three two-tree blocks.

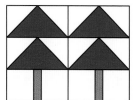

Make 3.

6. Sew a 2½" x 6½" tree background rectangle to each long edge of the remaining single-tree units. Press seams toward the background rectangles. Make three.

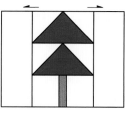

Make 3.

7. Sew the block sets from steps 5 and 6 together, alternating blocks. Referring to the quilt plan on page 75, note that the winter and summer panels start with a two-tree block and the spring and fall panels begin with a single-tree block. Press seams toward the background rectangles.

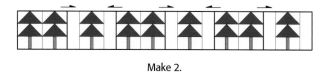

Make 2.

Make 2.

Making One Fence Row

1. Sew field and fence strips together into a strip set as shown. Press seams toward the fence strips. Make three sets.

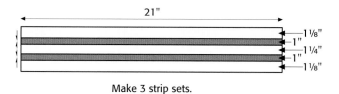

Make 3 strip sets.

2. Crosscut the strips into 10 rail sections, 4½" wide.

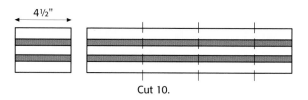

Cut 10.

3. Sew a 1¼" x 3½" fence-post rectangle between each of the 10 fence-rail units and add one to each end of the row as well. Press seams toward the fence posts.

4. Piece two 1½" field strips together. Cut to measure 48¾". Sew this strip to the top of the fence row. Press the seam toward the field row.

5. Trim ⅛" off each end of the row, or ease out seams if necessary, so that the row measures 48½".

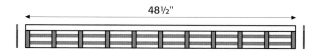

48½"

Assembling the Panels

1. Sew the mountain-and-sky row to the top of the tree row and the fence row to the bottom of the tree row. Press seams away from the tree row.

2. Repeat the preceding sections to make the three remaining panels.

3. Sew the four seasonal panels together. Press seams toward the sky fabric.

Adding the Borders

1. Sew the inner-border strips together end to end. Cut to make two strips that are 59" long and two that are 75" long. Repeat with the 3½" outer-border strips.

2. Sew each inner-border strip to an outer-border strip of the same length. Press seams toward the outer-border strips.

3. Referring to "Mitered Borders" on page 89, sew the borders to the quilt top.

Finishing Your Quilt

1. Layer the quilt top with batting and backing; baste.

2. Hand or machine quilt as desired.

3. Trim the batting and backing even with the quilt-top edges.

4. Referring to "French Binding" on page 92, prepare the 2" brown strips for binding and sew the binding to the quilt.

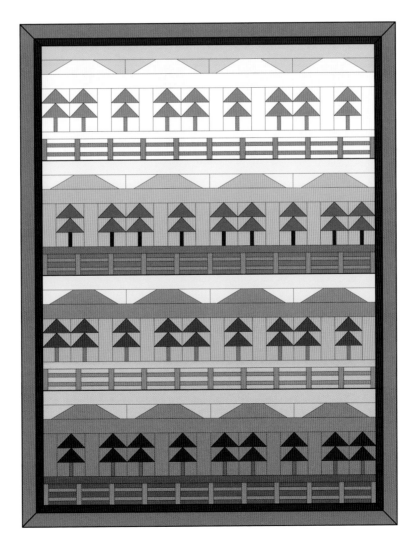

Postcards from Meadowbrook

Finished Size: 8" x 5½"

Here are a couple of "photographs" from my favorite sites along the Meadowbrook Loop. They'll make a great, quick project for a gift, or try making postcards to capture the beauty of your own favorite spot.

Materials (for one postcard)

5½" x 8" piece of sky fabric

Assorted scraps for appliqués (small-scale textured prints work well)

¼ yard of white for backing and binding

6" x 8½" piece of cotton batting

¼ yard of lightweight fusible web

6" x 8½" piece of lightweight fusible interfacing

6" x 8½" piece of freezer paper

Black fine-tip permanent marker

Small pair of sharp scissors

Appliqué press sheet (optional)

Fusible Appliqué

1. Trace the appliqué patterns onto the paper side of the fusible web, leaving at least ¾" between each shape. Please note that the appliqué patterns have been drawn in reverse to accommodate fusible appliqué.

2. Cut out the traced shapes, adding an approximate ¼" margin around each.

3. Place the shapes with the fusible web on the wrong side of the appropriate fabric, paper side up, and fuse following the manufacturer's directions.

4. Cut out the pieces on the traced lines and peel away the paper backing. Position the appliqués, right side up, on the 5½" x 8" sky piece. Place the pieces in numerical order, referring to the postcard layout for correct positioning. Fuse in place, following the manufacturer's directions. *NOTE:* Using an appliqué press sheet may be helpful in layering the individual pieces together prior to placing the design on the sky fabric. Follow product instructions.

Machine Quilting

1. Pin the fused postcard on top of the 6" x 8½" piece of batting. The backing will be added after the piece is quilted.

2. Using nylon monofilament thread, outline all of the appliqué shapes using a straight stitch and your machine.

3. To make the doors or fence wire (depending on which postcard image you are using), use black cotton thread and a straight stitch to add the details with your machine.

Making the Postcard Back

1. Cut a 6" x 8½" rectangle from the white fabric. Press the shiny side of the 6" x 8½" freezer paper to the wrong side of the white fabric. On the fabric side, use a permanent marker to draw the back of the postcard as shown.

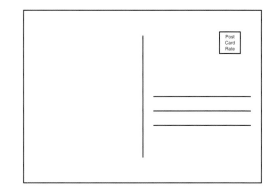

2. Add your own personal note if desired.

3. Remove the freezer paper from the back and replace it with the fusible lightweight interfacing. Fuse following the manufacturer's directions.

Finishing the Postcard

1. Pin the front of the postcard to the back with wrong sides together. Trim the card to measure 5½" x 8".

2. Cut a 1¼" x 42" strip from the white fabric. Referring to "Traditional Binding" on page 93, bind the postcard.

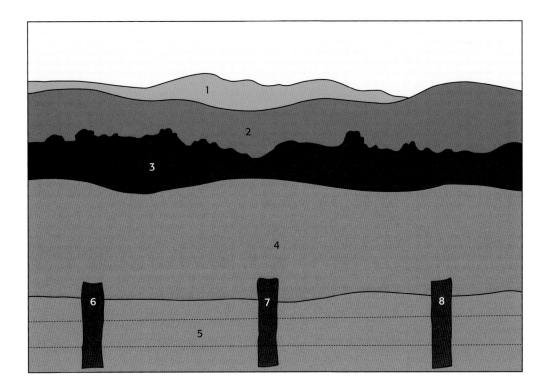

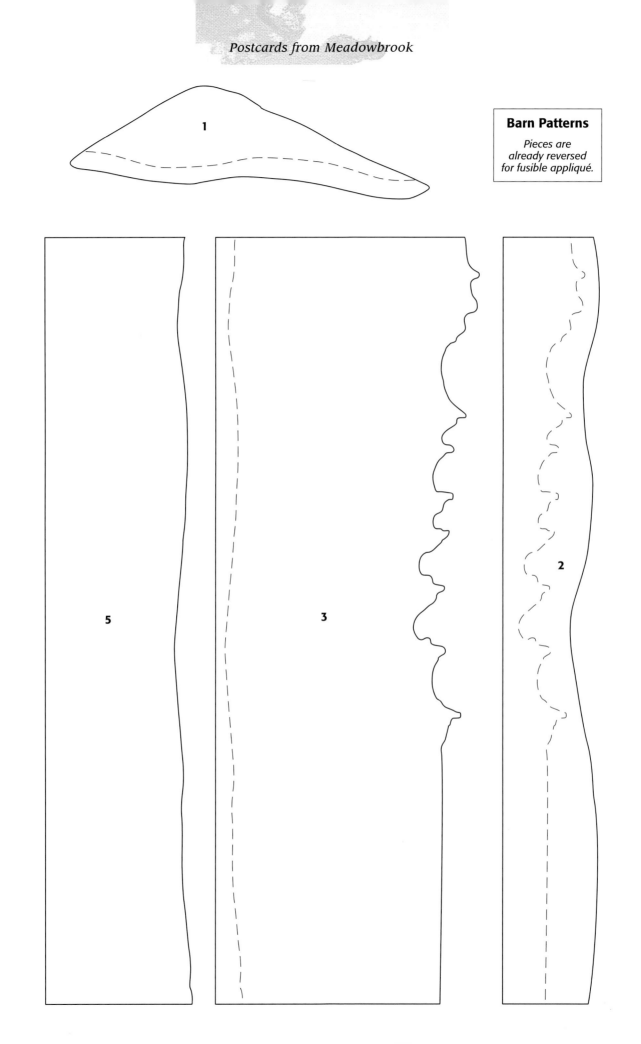

Barn Patterns

Pieces are already reversed for fusible appliqué.

1

5

3

2

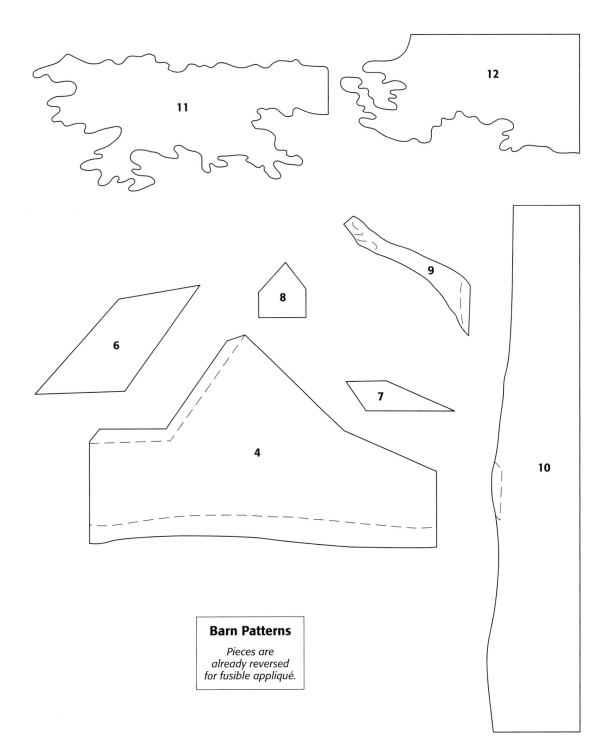

Barn Patterns

*Pieces are
already reversed
for fusible appliqué.*

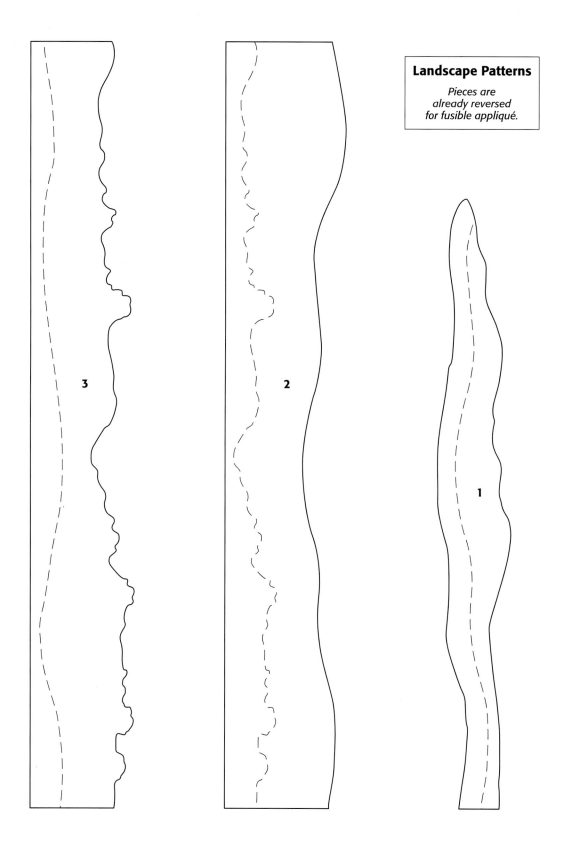

Landscape Patterns

*Pieces are
already reversed
for fusible appliqué.*

3

2

1

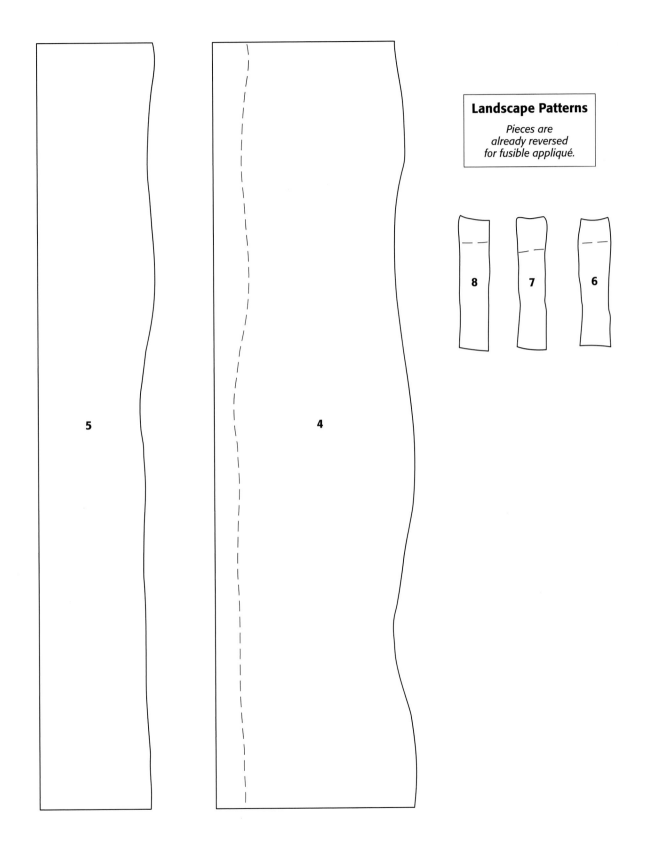

Landscape Patterns

*Pieces are
already reversed
for fusible appliqué.*

8

7

6

5

4

General Directions

This section includes helpful instructions for completing the projects in this book. To make sure that you are pleased with your finished quilt, stitch accurate ¼"-wide seam allowances and follow the pressing directions with each step before proceeding to the next step.

Appliquéing

The instructions that follow describe three appliqué methods: freezer-paper, needle-turn, and invisible machine appliqué.

Freezer-Paper Appliqué

With freezer-paper appliqué, a freezer-paper template stabilizes the appliqué piece during the entire process. You can easily remove the freezer paper by cutting away the backing fabric behind the completed appliqué.

1. Trace the appliqué patterns in reverse on the unwaxed (dull) side of the freezer paper. Cut out the templates on the traced lines.

2. Place the freezer-paper templates, shiny side down, on the wrong side of the chosen fabric and use a dry iron to attach them to the fabric. Leave at least ¾" of space between pieces when attaching more than one freezer-paper template to the same fabric.

3. Cut out each shape, adding a ¼" allowance beyond the template edges. Trim the allowances to ³⁄₁₆" after cutting out each one.

Clip inner curves, and trim points to eliminate bulk.

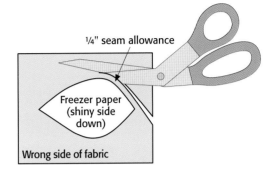

4. Turn the allowances over the freezer-paper edge and secure with hand basting through the paper and both fabric layers.

5. Pin or baste the appliqué on the background fabric and sew in place with an appliqué stitch (see "Hand Appliqué Stitch" on page 87). Remove the basting.

6. On the wrong side of the appliqué piece, cut away the background fabric, leaving a ¼" allowance all around. Remove the freezer paper, using your fingers, a needle, or tweezers to gently pull it away from the appliqué.

Needle-Turn Appliqué

Needle-turn appliqué is the most traditional and perhaps the most time-consuming appliqué method. If you love handwork, this is the method for you.

1. Trace the appliqué patterns (as printed) on the unwaxed (dull) side of the freezer paper. Cut out the templates on the traced lines.

2. Place the freezer-paper templates, shiny side down, on the right side of the chosen fabric and use a dry iron to attach them to the fabric. Leave at least ¾" of space between pieces when attaching more than one freezer-paper template to the same fabric.

3. Use a No. 2 pencil on light fabric, or a white or yellow pencil on dark fabric, to trace around each template.

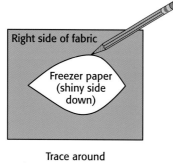

Trace around
freezer paper template.

4. Cut out the appliqués, adding a scant ¼" allowance all around. Peel away the appliqué template from each piece.

Cut out with ¼" seam allowance
all around.

5. Position the appliqués on the background fabric and pin or baste in place.

6. Starting at a straight area on one edge of each appliqué, use the tip of the needle to turn under the allowances along the marked line about ½" at a time. Clip the seam allowance as needed in curved areas. Sew in place with the hand appliqué stitch (see page 87).

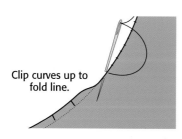

Clip curves up to
fold line.

Invisible Machine Appliqué

This is the quickest appliqué method. Use this method when the appliqué patterns are large and contain gentle curves. To prepare appliqué patterns for this method:

1. If you need multiple pattern shapes that are *symmetrical*, trace the pattern several times along one edge of a piece of freezer paper. Fold the paper back and forth to get three or four layers. Pin through all layers in the middle of each traced pattern and cut out on the traced line.

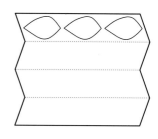

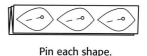

Pin each shape.

2. Place the freezer-paper template, dull side down, on the *wrong* side of the chosen fabric. Pin in place. Leave at least ¾" of space between pieces when cutting more than one freezer-paper template from the same fabric.

3. Cut out each shape, adding a generous ¼" allowance beyond the template edges.

4. Use the tip of a dry iron to press the appliqué seam allowance onto the shiny side of the paper. Smooth the seams around the template shapes, making sure there are no tucks on the front of the appliqué.

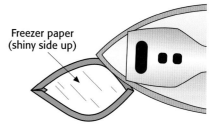

Freezer paper
(shiny side up)

5. Secure loose corners with a small dab of glue from a glue stick.

6. Pin the appliqué in place on the background fabric.

Invisible Machine Appliqué Stitch

Machine stitches that can be used for invisible machine appliqué will vary with the make and model of the machine used. The trick is to try to mimic the hand appliqué stitch using your machine.

1. Thread the top of your machine with invisible nylon monofilament thread. In the bobbin, use cotton thread or cotton-covered polyester thread to match the background fabric.

2. Attach an open-toe appliqué foot.

3. For the most basic sewing machine, use a zigzag stitch 1 mm to 1.5 mm long and about 1 mm wide. The blind hem stitch is another stitch that works well if you are able to adjust the length and width of the stitch. With my Bernina sewing machine, I've experienced the best results using the Vari-Lock stitch set in mirror image with a few adjustments to length and width. You will need to practice a little with your machine and see what works best for you.

4. Place your appliqué piece under the presser foot so that the left swing position of the needle will stitch into the appliqué, and the right swing position will stitch into the background.

Left swing position   Right swing position

5. Stitch around the piece, overlapping the starting point by a few stitches to secure.

6. On the wrong side of the appliqué piece, cut away the background fabric, leaving a generous ¼" allowance all around. Remove the freezer paper. If you are careful in removing the paper, you may be able to reuse the pattern a few more times. If it is difficult to remove, check to make sure that your stitches are not taking too big of a bite into the appliqué. Readjust the stitch width if necessary.

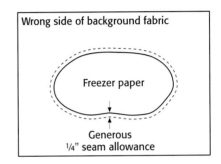

Hand Appliqué Stitch

Choose a long, thin needle, such as a Sharp or appliqué needle, for stitching.

1. Tie a knot in a single strand of thread that closely matches the appliqué color.

2. Bring the needle to the front from the wrong side of the appliqué. Bring the needle up on the fold line, and blindstitch along the folded edge. Take a stitch approximately every ⅛".

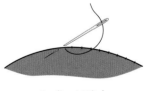

Appliqué Stitch

3. To end the stitching, pull the needle through to the wrong side. Take two small stitches, making knots by taking your needle through the loops.

Quick and Easy Flying Geese

The following method is an easy way to quickly make four flying-geese units at a time. Each unit is made up of two small squares from a background fabric and one large square that becomes the "geese" triangle (the large triangle in the middle).

1. On each of the smaller background squares, draw a light pencil line diagonally from corner to corner. To make it easier to mark the fabric, place the squares on the gritty side of a piece of very fine-grain sandpaper so they won't slip while you draw.

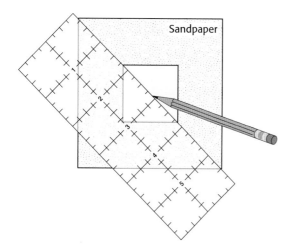

2. With right sides together, place the small background squares at opposite corners of the large square, aligning the edges. The background squares will slightly overlap in the center. Pin in place. Sew an accurate ¼" seam on each side of the drawn lines.

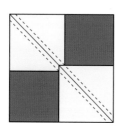

3. Cut the square in half diagonally on the drawn line. Flip the small triangles open and press the seams toward them.

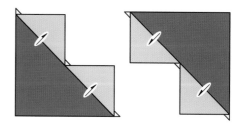

4. Position another small square in the corner of each of the two units from step 3 as shown. Sew an accurate ¼" seam on each side of the drawn line.

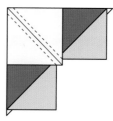

5. Cut on the pencil lines to create two flying-geese units from each triangle. Press toward the small triangles.

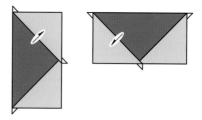

6. Repeat steps 1–5 to make the required number of flying-geese units for your project.

Adding Borders

This section describes the most basic directions for making borders. Slight variations of this method may appear throughout this book due to the nature of the border design.

Straight-Cut Borders

1. Measure the length of the quilt top through the center. Cut border strips to this measurement, piecing as necessary. Mark the center of the quilt edges and border strips. Pin the border strips to the sides of the quilt top, matching the center marks and ends and easing as necessary. Sew the border strips in place. Press the seams toward the border.

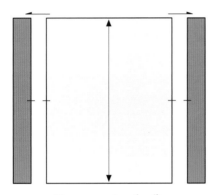

Measure center of quilt,
top to bottom. Mark centers.

2. Measure the width of the quilt top through the center, including the side border strips just added. Cut border strips to this measurement, piecing as necessary. Mark the center of the quilt edges and the border strips. Pin the border strips to the top and bottom edges of the quilt top, matching the center marks and ends and easing as necessary; stitch. Press the seams toward the border.

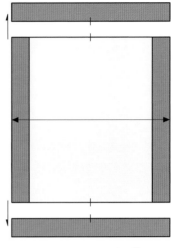

Measure center of quilt,
side to side, including borders.
Mark centers.

Mitered Borders

Strips for mitered borders are cut extra long and trimmed to fit after stitching the mitered corners.

1. To add a border with mitered corners, measure the quilt top through the center and mark this length on the border with a pin at each end. Pin-mark the center of the strip. Pin the border strip to the edge, matching the border strip to the quilt-top center, with the pins at the ends. An even amount of excess border strip should extend beyond each end of the quilt top.

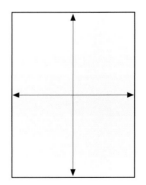

2. Stitch, beginning and ending the seam ¼" from the quilt-top corners. Repeat with the remaining border strips.

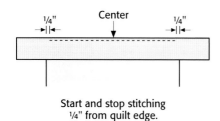

Start and stop stitching
¼" from quilt edge.

3. Working on a flat surface, place one border on top of the other at a 90° angle.

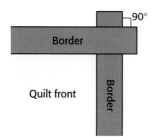

4. Turn the top border layer back at a 45° angle and press to mark the stitching line.

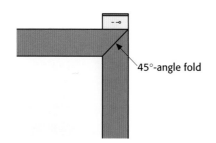

45°-angle fold

5. With right sides together, pin the borders together. Begin stitching at the inner corner, sewing on the crease and backstitching as you begin and end the stitching.

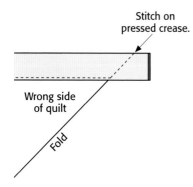

Stitch on
pressed crease.

Wrong side
of quilt

Fold

6. Trim away the excess border fabric, leaving a ¼"-wide seam allowance. Press the seam open. Repeat with the remaining corners.

Trim mitered seams
and press open.

Layering the Quilt

The quilt "sandwich" consists of the backing, batting, and quilt top. I recommend cutting the quilt backing at least 4" larger than the quilt top all around. For large quilts, it is usually necessary to sew two or three lengths of fabric together to make a backing of the required size. Trim away the selvage edges (they are more difficult to quilt through) before sewing the lengths together. Press the backing seams open to make quilting easier.

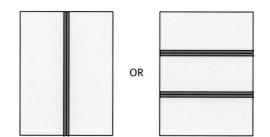

OR

1. Spread the backing, wrong side up, on a flat clean surface. Anchor it with pins or masking tape. Be careful not to stretch the backing out of shape.

2. Spread the batting over the backing, smoothing out any wrinkles.

3. Place the pressed quilt top, right side up, on top of the batting. Smooth out any wrinkles and make sure the edges of the quilt top are parallel to the edges of the backing.

4. For hand quilting, start in the center and hand baste the layers together in a grid of horizontal and vertical lines spaced 6" to 8" apart. Baste around the outer edges of the quilt top.

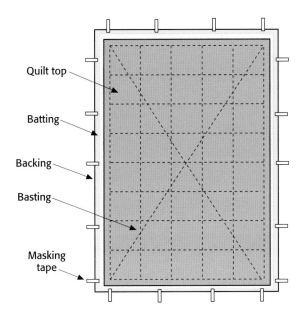

Quilt top

Batting

Backing

Basting

Masking tape

For machine quilting, pin the layers together using #1, nickel-plated safety pins. Begin pinning the center, working toward the outside edges and placing pins every 3" to 4" throughout.

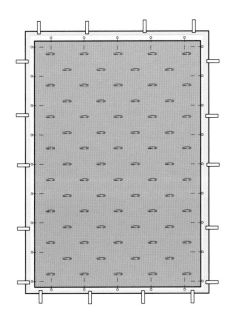

Quilting

All of the large projects in this book were professionally machine quilted by Joanne Case. Feel free to choose your favorite method for quilting your project.

The following are a few tips for quilting by machine:

- Machine quilting is suitable for all quilt types, from crib- to full-size bed quilts. With machine quilting you can quickly complete quilts that might otherwise languish on your shelves.

- For straight-line quilting, it is extremely helpful to have a walking foot to feed the quilt layers through the machine without shifting or puckering. Some machines have a built-in walking foot or even-feed feature; other machines require a separate attachment.

Walking Foot

- Use free-motion quilting to outline a quilt pattern in the fabric or to create stippling and many other curved designs. You will need a darning foot and the ability to drop the feed dogs on your machine. Instead of turning the fabric to change directions, you guide the fabric in the direction of the design, using the needle like a pencil.

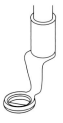

Darning Foot

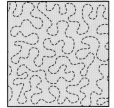

Binding

Two different types of binding are used in this book. For the larger quilts, French binding was used for its durability and ease of application. Traditional binding was used on the small quilt projects and the wool quilt to reduce bulk.

French Binding

To make straight-cut, double-layer binding, also known as French binding, cut strips 2" wide, cutting across the fabric width. You will need enough strips to go around the perimeter of the quilt, plus 10" for seams and the corners in the mitered folds.

1. With right sides together, sew the strips together on the diagonal as shown to create one long strip. Trim excess fabric and press the seams open.

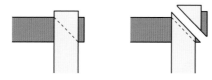

2. Cut one end at a 45° angle. Turn this end under ¼" and press. Fold the strip in half lengthwise, wrong sides together, and press.

Fold line

3. Trim the batting and backing even with the quilt-top edges, making sure the corners are square.

4. Beginning along one edge of the quilt and using a ¼"-wide seam allowance, start stitching about 3" from the beginning of the binding. Keep the raw edges even with the quilt edge. End the stitching ¼" from the corner of the quilt and backstitch.

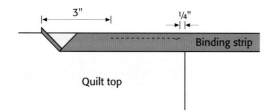

3"   ¼"

Binding strip

Quilt top

5. Fold the binding up, away from the quilt, and then back down onto itself, aligning the raw edges with the quilt-top edge. Begin stitching at the edge, backstitching to secure, and end ¼" from the lower edge. Repeat on the remaining edges.

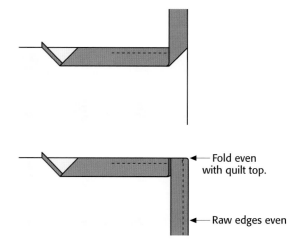

Fold even with quilt top.

Raw edges even

6. When you reach the beginning of the binding, lap the strip over the beginning end by about 1" and cut away any excess binding. Trim the end at a 45° angle. Tuck the end of the binding into the fold and complete the seam.

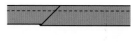

7. Fold the binding over the raw edges of the quilt to the back, with the folded edge just covering the machine stitching. Blindstitch into place, including the miter that forms at each corner.

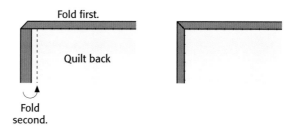

Fold first.

Quilt back

Fold second.

Traditional Binding

To make single-layer traditional binding, cut strips following the individual pattern instructions. Cut the strips across the fabric width. You will need enough strips to go around the perimeter of the quilt, plus 10" for seams and the corners in the mitered folds.

1. With right sides together, sew the strips together on the diagonal as shown in step 1 of "French Binding" on page 92. Trim excess fabric and press the seams open.

2. Fold the strip in half lengthwise, wrong sides together, and press. Open the strip. Fold each of the cut edges to meet the center crease, and press the new folds.

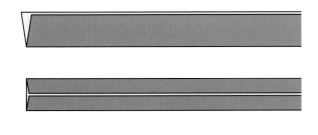

3. Open the folds of the binding. Cut one end at a 45° angle. Turn this end under ¼" and press. With right sides together, open the binding and place along the edge of the quilt.

Sew through all layers, using the first crease as your stitch guide. End the stitching ¼" from the corner of the quilt and backstitch.

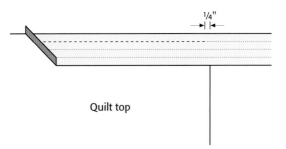

Quilt top

4. Sew the mitered corners, following the directions in step 5 of "French Binding" on page 92.

5. When you reach the beginning of the binding, lap the strip over the beginning stitches by about 1" and cut away excess binding. Stitch the overlap to complete the seam.

6. Fold the binding over the edge of the quilt. Blindstitch the pressed edge of the binding to the back of the quilt, including the miter that forms at the corners of the quilt.

About the Author

Photo by Mystique Photography

Jean Van Bockel started quilting in 1986 when she joined a quilt group in Snohomish, Washington. She feels fortunate to have learned from so many accomplished quilters over the years and attributes much of her skill and knowledge to her current quilt group, the Out to Lunch Bunch.

Jean has taught beginning quilting and appliqué classes, and she is well known for her creative design ability and award-winning quilts.

She has written one other book for Martingale & Company, *Quilts from Larkspur Farm,* with Pamela Mostek.

Jean and her husband, Mark, live in Coeur d' Alene, Idaho, and are the parents of three grown children. Many family dogs have accompanied Jean on her walks along Meadowbrook Loop, but her current walking companion is Foster, an Australian shepherd. As with the postman, neither rain, nor snow, nor sleet, nor hail will keep this dog from the trail!

new and bestselling titles from

America's Best-Loved Craft & Hobby Books®

America's Best-Loved Quilt Books®

NEW RELEASES
20 Decorated Baskets
Asian Elegance
Batiks and Beyond
Classic Knitted Vests
Clever Quilts Encore
Crocheted Socks!
Four Seasons of Quilts
Happy Endings
Judy Murrah's Jacket Jackpot
Knits for Children and Their Teddies
Loving Stitches
Meadowbrook Quilts
Once More around the Block
Pairing Up
Patchwork Memories
Pretty and Posh
Professional Machine Quilting
Purely Primitive
Shadow Appliqué
Snowflake Follies
Style at Large
Trashformations
World of Quilts, A

APPLIQUÉ
Appliquilt in the Cabin
Artful Album Quilts
Blossoms in Winter
Color-Blend Appliqué
Garden Party
Sunbonnet Sue All through the Year

HOLIDAY QUILTS & CRAFTS
Christmas Cats and Dogs
Christmas Delights
Creepy Crafty Halloween
Handcrafted Christmas, A
Hocus Pocus!
Make Room for Christmas Quilts
Snowman's Family Album Quilt, A
Welcome to the North Pole

LEARNING TO QUILT
101 Fabulous Rotary-Cut Quilts
Casual Quilter, The
Fat Quarter Quilts
More Fat Quarter Quilts
Quick Watercolor Quilts
Quilts from Aunt Amy
Simple Joys of Quilting, The
Your First Quilt Book (or it should be!)

PAPER PIECING
40 Bright and Bold Paper-Pieced Blocks
50 Fabulous Paper-Pieced Stars
Down in the Valley
Easy Machine Paper Piecing
For the Birds
It's Raining Cats and Dogs
Papers for Foundation Piecing
Quilter's Ark, A
Show Me How to Paper Piece
Traditional Quilts to Paper Piece

QUILTS FOR BABIES & CHILDREN
Easy Paper-Pieced Baby Quilts
Even More Quilts for Baby
More Quilts for Baby
Play Quilts
Quilts for Baby
Sweet and Simple Baby Quilts

ROTARY CUTTING/SPEED PIECING
101 Fabulous Rotary-Cut Quilts
365 Quilt Blocks a Year Perpetual Calendar
1000 Great Quilt Blocks
Around the Block Again
Around the Block with Judy Hopkins
Cutting Corners
Log Cabin Fever
Pairing Up
Strips and Strings
Triangle-Free Quilts
Triangle Tricks

SCRAP QUILTS
Nickel Quilts
Rich Traditions
Scrap Frenzy
Spectacular Scraps
Successful Scrap Quilts

TOPICS IN QUILTMAKING
Americana Quilts
Bed and Breakfast Quilts
Bright Quilts from Down Under
Creative Machine Stitching
Everyday Embellishments
Fabulous Quilts from Favorite Patterns
Folk Art Friends
Handprint Quilts
Just Can't Cut It!
Quilter's Home: Winter, The
Split-Diamond Dazzlers
Time to Quilt

CRAFTS
300 Papermaking Recipes
ABCs of Making Teddy Bears, The
Blissful Bath, The
Creating with Paint
Handcrafted Frames
Handcrafted Garden Accents
Painted Whimsies
Pretty and Posh
Sassy Cats
Stamp in Color

KNITTING & CROCHET
365 Knitting Stitches a Year
    Perpetual Calendar
Basically Brilliant Knits
Crochet for Tots
Crocheted Aran Sweaters
Knitted Sweaters for Every Season
Knitted Throws and More
Knitter's Template, A
Knitting with Novelty Yarns
More Paintbox Knits
Simply Beautiful Sweaters for Men
Today's Crochet
Too Cute! Cotton Knits for Toddlers
Treasury of Rowan Knits, A
Ultimate Knitter's Guide, The

Our books are available at bookstores and your favorite craft, fabric, and yarn retailers. If you don't see the title you're looking for, visit us at **www.martingale-pub.com** or contact us at:

1-800-426-3126

International: 1-425-483-3313 • Fax: 1-425-486-7596 • Email: info@martingale-pub.com

For more information and a full list of our titles, visit our Web site.